The **Chan**
Handbook

II

Venerable Master Hua

IV

The
CHAN
HANDBOOK

Talks about Meditation by
Venerable Master Hua

English translation &
Published by the

Buddhist Text Translation Society

The Chan Handbook

Published and Translated by:

The Buddhist Text Translation Society
4951 Bodhi Way, Ukiah, CA 95482

© 2004   Buddhist Text Translation Society
            Dharma Realm Buddhist Association
            Dharma Realm Buddhist University

Printed in Malaysia

Addresses Dharma Realm Buddhist Association branch addresses are listed at the back of this book.

Library of Congress Cataloging-in-Publication Data
Hsuan Hua, 1918-The Chan handbook: talks about meditation /by Venerable Master Hsuan Hua. p.cm.

ISBN 0-88139-951-5 (hard : alk. paper)
1. Meditation--Zen Buddhism. I. Title: Talks about meditation. II. Title.

BQ9288.H76 2005
294.3'4435--dc22

2004010894

Contents

XIII

XIV

Selected Preface

By Elder Master De Ching Hsu Yun of Jen Ru Monastery, on Yun Ju mountain, in the province of Jiang-Xi, the Forty-fourth Patriarch in India, the Seventeenth Patriarch in China, and the Eighth Patriarch in the Wei Yang Lineage.

Put everything down.
Let no thought arise.

A Talk by Elder Master Hsu Yun

The goal of investigating Chan is to understand the mind and see the true nature. That is, to remove all the defilements in our minds and to actually see the image of our self-nature. Defilements refer to false thoughts and attachments, while the self-nature refers to our inherent wisdom and virtue, which is identical to that of all Buddhas. The Thus Come Ones' wisdom and virtue is embodied within all Buddhas and sentient beings and is not dual or different. Anyone who can be apart from false thoughts and attachments can certify to the Thus Come Ones' wisdom and virtue and become a Buddha. Otherwise, we remain ordinary sentient beings.

Immeasurable eons ago we became caught in the cycle of birth and death. By now, we have been defiled for so long that we cannot just suddenly get rid of our false thoughts and see our original nature. That is why we have to investigate Chan. Therefore, the first step in investigating Chan is to eliminate false thoughts. How can false thoughts be eliminated? Sakyamuni Buddha talked a lot about this. The easiest method is none other than ceasing. The saying goes: ceasing is Bodhi. The Chan School was transmitted to China by Great Master Bodhidharma, who became the first patriarch. That transmission continued, being received eventually by the Sixth Patriarch.

Thereafter, the teaching of Chan spreads far and wide. Through the ages, its impact has been tremendous. However, the teaching given by Venerable Bodhidharma and the Sixth Patriarch is considered the most important. It is, in essence, making everything still and then not letting a single thought arise. Making everything still means putting everything down. Those two phrases of putting everything down, and not letting a thought arise are the essential requisites for investigating Chan. If we fail to meet these two requirements, then we will not be able to master the rudiments of Chan, how much the less succeed in investigating Chan. How can any of us say we are investigating Chan when we are still covered over and bound by the myriad conditions, and our thoughts come into being and cease to be without interruption?

Put everything down. Let no thought arise. Those are the requisites for investigating Chan. Since we know this, how can we achieve them? First, we need to put each and every thought to rest until no more arise. Doing that, we will certify to Bodhi instantly without any trouble. Second, we need to be reasonable in dealing with all matters and to fully understand that the self-nature is originally pure and clear. We need to realize that affliction, Bodhi, birth, death, and nirvana are all merely names and, as such, have nothing to do with our self-nature. All material objects are like dreams and illusions, bubbles and shadows. In the scope of our self-nature, our bodies and our environment, both of which are composed of the four elements, are just like bubbles that randomly form and vanish in the sea, without affecting the original substance. We should not get caught up in the coming into being, dwelling, changes, and ceasing to be of the illusory things in this world. Nor should we indulge in fondness and dislike, grasping and rejecting. By totally disregarding this body, just as if we were a dead person, we will naturally reduce the effect of being tainted by our sense faculties and our mind consciousness. In that way, we will be able to eliminate greed, hatred, ignorance, and emotional love. We will no longer be influenced by pain and pleasure this body experiences, including hunger and cold, satiation and warmth, honor and humiliation, life and death, misfortune and blessings, good or ill luck, slander and praise, gain and loss, safety and danger.

At that point, we will have achieved putting down. If, in putting things down, we can do so totally and permanently, then we will have achieved putting everything down. When we have put everything down, false thoughts will naturally vanish, discriminations will no longer be made, and we will be far apart from attachments. At the point when not a single thought arises, the light of our self-nature will manifest completely, and we will then naturally have fulfilled the requirements for investigating Chan. It is only by diligently applying our skill in investigation that we have the chance of understanding our mind and seeing our true nature.

Recently, many Chan practitioners have come to ask questions. There is actually no Dharma to speak because what can be expressed in words or commented upon in language will not be the true meaning. Always remember that our mind was originally the Buddha. All along, it has continued to be inherent in each of us. Self-declarations about cultivation and certification amount to the words of demons. When Venerable Bodhidharma came to China, he pointed directly at people's minds as the way to see their nature and become Buddhas. In this way, he clearly indicated that all sentient beings on earth have the Buddha nature. We need to recognize that this pure and clear self-nature accords with conditions without being defiled. We need to realize that in every moment, in everything we do, our true mind is no different from that of the Buddhas. If we certify to that, then we will have become a Buddha right here and now. Once we certify to that, then there will be no need for any further mental or physical exertion. We will not need to talk, to think, or to do anything at all. In that sense, becoming a Buddha is actually the easiest and most comfortable thing to do.

Sentient beings need only wish not to revolve continually in the cycle of the four types of rebirth in the six realms of existence, where they are always sinking in the sea of suffering. If sentient beings wish to become Buddhas and to attain the eternity, joy, true self, and purity of nirvana, then they should truly and sincerely believe in the Buddha's teachings, put everything down, and stop having thoughts of good or evil. By doing that, each of us can become Buddhas. All Buddhas and Bodhisattvas, as well as all patriarchs through the ages, have vowed to save all sentient beings. This is not without basis or evidence. They did not make great vows for nothing, nor were they engaging in false speech.

Verse in Expression of Faith from Dhyana Master Hsu Yun

Proclaiming [Hsuan] Wei's wonderful meaning,
Causes the sect's teaching to be echoed far and wide.
The transformations [Hua] inherited from Ling Peak
Exalt the Dharma Path.
Taking Across [Du] the forty-sixth,
The mind seal is transmitted.
The wheel [Lun] revolves unceasingly,
Rescuing the suffering hordes.

"Year of the Buddha" 2983, the year Bingshen
Written by De Qing Hsu Yun, the eighth generation of the Wei Yang,
at the Dharma Lecture Hall of Zhenru Chan Monastery

XXIII

Biography of
Master Hsuan Hua

The Venerable Master Hsuan Hua was also known as An Tse and To Lun. The name Hsuan Hua was bestowed upon him after he received the transmission of the Wei Yang Lineage of the Chan School from Venerable Elder Hsu Yun. He left the home life at the age of nineteen. After the death of his mother, he lived in a tiny thatched hut by her grave for three years, as an act of filial respect. During that time, he practiced meditation and studied the Buddha's teachings. Among his many practices were eating only once at midday and never lying down to sleep.

In 1948, the Master arrived in Hong Kong, where he founded the Buddhist Lecture Hall and other monasteries. In 1962, he brought the Proper Dharma to America and the West, where he lectured extensively on the major works of the Mahayana Buddhist canon and

XXV

XXVI

established the Dharma Realm Buddhist Association, as well as the City of Ten Thousand Buddhas, the International Translation Institute, various other monastic facilities, Dharma Realm Buddhist University, Developing Virtue Secondary School, Instilling Goodness Elementary School, the vocational Sangha and Laity Training Programs, and other education centers.

The Master passed into stillness on June 7, 1995, in Los Angeles, California, USA, causing many people throughout the world to mourn the sudden setting of the sun of wisdom. Although his life has passed on, his lofty example will always be remembered. Throughout his life he worked selflessly and vigorously to benefit the people of the world and all living beings. His wisdom and compassion inspired many to correct their faults and lead wholesome lives. Here we include the Records of the Mendicant of Chang Bai written by the Venerable Master. This verse serves as a model for all of us to emulate.

> *The monk from Long White Mountain,*
> *simple and honest by nature,*
> *Was always quick to help people*
> *and benefit others.*
> *Forgetting himself for the Dharma,*
> *he made lifelong sacrifices.*
> *Dispensing cures for people's ills,*
> *he spared not his marrow and blood.*

His vow was to join in substance
  all the millions of different beings.
His practices swelled to fill space itself,
  as he gathered in all with potentials.
Unhindered by mundane distinctions
  of past, future, and present,
His scope reached beyond the confines
  of north, south, east, or west.

~composed by Master Hua

1. Why Investigate Chan?

When thoughts cease,
confusion ends.

We humans are born confused and die confused. We are confused while asleep and confused while awake. What value is there in that kind of life?

So does that mean that we do not want to be human beings anymore? No, but we have to understand where we came from when we were born and where we will go after death. Someone may say, "I know how to find out about death. I can overdose on drugs or hang myself or jump into a river. Would I not know then?" Suicide will not free you from birth and death. It will only increase your karmic burden.

We sit in meditation in order to find a way to ensure that, when it is time for us to die, we will not suffer physical sickness, we will not crave wealth, sex, fame, food and sleep, and our minds will not be upside down. Death should be just as if we had entered into Chan samadhi. We want to pass away with a smile, be without discomfort, and have Amitabha Buddha welcome us with a golden dais. We want to be able to predict our own passing and to know of its coming in advance. We want to know the year, month, day and even the precise time when we will pass away once all our tasks have been completed.

Cultivation is just for that purpose! If we do not know about that crucial moment, then we will remain confused throughout our entire life. Nor will that confusion end with death. In death after death we will still be confused. In life after life we will be unclear. How pitiful to be perpetually confused.

The reason we practice sitting in meditation and want to learn Buddhism is because we do not want to be confused. Many people spend their time doing scientific research aimed at trying to determine the makeup and workings of the physical body so that they can reproduce it. Those who seek scientific solutions outside themselves are forsaking the roots and going after the branch tips. When we understand our original self, we will then gain great wisdom. Learning Buddhism will allow that great wisdom to unfold.

Freedom over birth and death is freedom to come and go.

Those who investigate Chan can become masters over their own birth and death. They can come and go freely without any restriction. As it is said,

My destiny is determined by me,
not by heaven.

Even Old Man Yama will no longer have control over us! Why not? We will have transcended the Three Realms.

What does freedom to come and go involve? It refers to freedom to be born and to die. If we want to live, we can live. If we want to die, we can die. The choice will be ours, as we wish. Please take note, however, that this kind of death does not mean committing suicide.

This freedom allows us to relate to our physical body as we would our house. If we want to go out and travel, we will be free to go wherever we want. If we

4

wish, we can have a hundred million transformation bodies to teach sentient beings throughout empty space and the Dharma Realm. If we do not wish to travel, we can stay in the house and no one will disturb us.

We should know that everything in empty space and in the Dharma Realm is included within the Dharma-body. Nothing can go outside the Dharma-body.

All of you have gone to a lot of trouble to attend this Chan session, and to work non-stop day and night. You are doing this because you hope to gain freedom and security over birth and death. You want to control your own life and to be your own master. Being able to do that is truly the state of freedom over birth and death.

In investigating Chan, you need to reach the state of not knowing that there is sky above, earth below, and people in between. You need to become one with empty space. Then there is some hope for enlightenment.

Right now, walking and sitting, sitting and walking provide the key that will open our wisdom.

The great functioning of
the entire substance is clearly
understood.

If we do not investigate Chan and do not practice sitting in meditation, we will continue not to know where we came from at birth and where we will go after death. Not knowing those things, we will again be born and die in confusion. To keep living lives in that manner is indeed pitiful!

Those who work hard at Chan practice can awaken and recognize who they were before their parents gave birth to them. They will suddenly see everything very clearly. They will understand in fine detail the ins and outs of all matters. They will fathom the great functioning of the true mind. Those who realize such a state are destined to attain the fruition of Buddhahood. In the future they will attain unsurpassed, right and equal enlightenment.

By investigating Chan and sitting in meditation, we can gain enlightenment.

How do we get enlightened? Enlightenment is like unlocking a door that has been restricting our entry and exit. We need a key to unlock that door. Without a key, we will remain locked up in this room forever. So, where is the key? It is right there with you. It is very easy to find.

How will you find it? You can do so by investigating Chan and sitting in meditation, or by chanting the Buddhas' names and holding mantras. Practicing in those ways is equivalent to searching for the key.

When will you find it? That depends on your stage of cultivation. If you practice with vigor and fortitude, you will find it very quickly. But if you are lazy and lethargic, you will never find it, not just in this life, but even in future lives you will not find it. This is a very simple principle.

We want to learn how not to be attached to self and others.

All things come to life
Each time spring returns.
Shatter empty space.
Be free and at ease.

Break attachments.
Let self and others go.
Expand to fill the Dharma Realm,
However vast that is.

When we investigate Chan, we have the chance to be enlightened. The brightness of our self-nature will shine forth just as when spring returns to the great earth and everything comes to life again. Empty space is originally without shape. When even this shapeless void has been shattered, one becomes free. From then onwards, one no longer attaches to the mark of others or the mark of self. The Dharma Realm may be large but we can still encompass it. Having done that, will we not be great heroes?

Meditation and samadhi are vital to our Dharma-body.

Sitting in meditation and cultivating samadhi is like feeding our Dharma-body. The physical body needs to be fed and clothed, needs to sleep, and is always busy working to achieve these needs. One cannot go without food, clothes, and sleep for even one day. Everyone is the same in this respect. We cannot do without any one of these things.

But our Dharma-body also needs food, clothes, and sleep. Sitting in meditation provides our Dharma-body with natural food. By absorbing the true nutrients from empty space, our Dharma-body will thrive. Entering samadhi gives our Dharma-body essential rest. If we never enter samadhi, our Dharma-body gets no rest. And finally, our Dharma-body must be clothed in tolerance.

Meditation and samadhi are vital to our

Dharma-body. When we meditate long enough, our Dharma-body will taste the flavor of Dharma and can absorb the true goodness of empty space.

The physical body needs these three items, and so does the Dharma-body. When we cultivate, we should clothe our Dharma-body in our own tolerance. We should enter the Thus Come One's abode by entering samadhi. And ultimately we should ascend to the Thus Come One's seat. This is how we should nurture the Dharma-body every day.

Sitting long brings Chan, which cleanses and purifies the mind.

The aim of sitting in meditation is to open our wisdom. Enlightenment is the opening of our wisdom. With wisdom, we will no longer be confused, the way we have been in the past. If we sit without moving and our mind does not wander, we can enter samadhi. When we have samadhi, our wisdom will naturally open up and all our problems will be solved effortlessly.

The Buddha is not very different from an ordinary person. The difference is that he has great wisdom. Great wisdom accesses spiritual penetrations whereupon the mind and spirit have no obstruction. Wisdom and spiritual penetrations are dual and yet non-dual, but they are not the supernatural power of ghosts. Ghostly penetrations arise from using the perceptive minds' deduction. Ghosts may think that they are intelligent, but they are not. Real wisdom does not require thinking.

11

When we gain real wisdom, our knowledge of things comes naturally, and we can exercise it freely. When we have wisdom, we fully understand all things. Without wisdom, all things become upside-down. Things may be upside-down, yet one who lacks wisdom is still unaware of that. If one knows one's mistakes, one may still be saved. However, if one was unaware of one's mistakes, what results will bring real suffering!

If we want to leave suffering and gain happiness, we must have wisdom. With wisdom, we need not suffer anymore. If we understand this principle, we can avoid any more afflictions. Actually, this reasoning is very simple. However, Chan sitting requires time. As it is said,

> *Practice sitting for a long time and*
> *Chan will appear.*
> *Live in one place a long time and*
> *Affinities will develop.*

Investigating Chan actually cleanses and purifies our minds. Stilling thoughts is a process of calming down our thoughts and getting rid of all the defilements. This is exactly what Venerable Master Shen Xiu meant when he said,

> *Time and again brush it clean;*
> *And let no dust alight.*

If we understand this principle, we should make determined effort in our practice of Chan. Everyone must strive hard and be patient. Though our legs may get sore and our back may ache, we must endure that pain. Remember,

> *If the plum tree did not endure cold*
>   *that chills to the bone,*
> *How could the fragrance*
>   *of its blossoms be so sweet?*

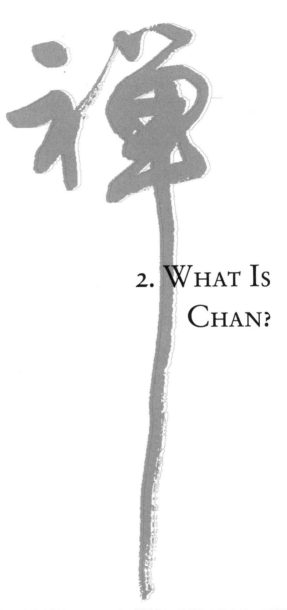

2. WHAT IS CHAN?

Concentrating on a focal point is the key to success in everything.

The method of sitting in meditation is essential to learn in cultivation. What does the word Chan mean? Chan is a Chinese abbreviation for the Sanskrit word, Dhyana. Dhyana means thought cultivation that leads to stilling our thoughts. Chan meditation is the method used to reach Dhyana, a stilling of our thoughts.

Normally, when we sit, our minds wander. Where do our minds go? They indulge in false thinking, which sends us anywhere our thoughts take us. Without having to pay for traveling, we can take a rocket trip. The false thoughts fly everywhere without restraint. Why is it people do not have wisdom? It is because the mind wanders about. Why do we age day-by-day? It is because the mind rushes to all sorts of places.

Suppose someone drives a new car recklessly and aimlessly. Doing that will definitely consume and waste

15

a lot of fuel. Eventually, the car and its parts will be damaged and mechanical difficulties will result. This analogy applies to the human body as well. If we do not know how to take good care of it, if we indulge it without restraint, it will definitely consume a lot of 'fuel'. What 'fuel' would that be? That fuel is our precious mental energy. No matter how many times we refuel, we keep using it up.

Take for example people who consume tonics everyday, thinking that they are replenishing their bodies with nutrients. If people do not treasure their mental energy and are self-indulgent, then no matter how much tonic they consume, they will never replenish the wasted energy. As a proverb says, "Concentrating on a focal point is the key to success in everything."

We have to gather our thoughts and concentrate on a focal point. Then we will not deplete our mental energy. In other words, if we know how to drive well, we will not drive around recklessly and meet with an accident. Our car will also last longer. Similarly, if we know how to take care of ourselves, then it is possible to neither age nor die.

Twirling a flower, the Buddha revealed the mind-to-mind seal.

Shakyamuni Buddha initiated Chan investigation when he held aloft a flower in the Vulture Peak Assembly to indicate the transmission of the subtle and wonderful mind-seal Dharma door. At that time, Patriarch Mahakasyapa understood the intention of the Buddha, and smiled broadly. From then on, the mind-seal Dharma door of the Buddhas and Patriarchs was transmitted. Actually, Patriarch Mahakasyapa was already over a hundred years old and because he vigorously practiced asceticism, he normally would not have smiled. On this occasion, his smile was an indication that he had just received the Buddha's mind-to-mind seal.

Only quiet contemplation
can initiate Chan.

Chan means stilling thoughts. We will only realize Chan if we still our thoughts. Samadhi means not moving. If we move, we have no samadhi.

By taking Dharma bliss as food, Chan samadhi will manifest. When we cultivate the Way, we practice sitting in meditation. To develop Chan, we need to sit down. As we sit in meditation, our skill will manifest.

It should not be the case that as soon as you sit in meditation you fall asleep. This is not Chan sitting; this is Chan sleeping. Sleeping is not Chan and neither is it samadhi. In Chan, you cannot sleep. The bliss of Chan samadhi is different from sleeping when once you enter samadhi. When you are sleeping, you have already lost your senses and spiritual awareness. Without any awareness, you sleep confusedly, not knowing anything at all. Entering samadhi requires one to sit in an upright posture. One sits with a straight back and holds the head straight without nodding or inclining the neck.

What is meant by samadhi power? Samadhi has a certain power that supports and maintains your body in an upright posture so that you do not lean forward or tilt backward. Sitting upright effortlessly, you can enter Chan samadhi. In the midst of samadhi, there is an unimaginable joy that is inexplicable and indescribable. Because it surpasses what your mind can imagine, it is described like this:

> *The path of words and speech is cut off.*
> *The place of the mind's activity is gone.*

In Chan samadhi, you will experience a bliss that is continuous and unceasing. Experiencing the bliss of Chan samadhi inspires in us courage and vigor that surpasses the ordinary. That kind of courage and vigor is extremely strong and powerful. No other forces can overcome that type of power.

Thought cultivation
eliminates false thinking.

Chan sitting is also known as thought cultivation. From this definition, we know that it is impossible not to have false thinking during Chan sitting. Normally, our false thinking comes and goes just like waves on water. Waves come up because of wind. When we meditate, why do false thoughts arise? It is because our self-nature still contains falsehood. This falsehood is like the wind, and false thoughts are like waves stirred by the wind.

As we practice meditation, we need to silence our thoughts. That means we must stop the false winds.

Thought cultivation aims at reducing false thoughts and stopping the waves that constantly arise in our minds. Stilling means quieting the thoughts so they cease their movement. When we cease thinking and deliberating, we can give rise to samadhi power. Over time, as samadhi power develops, wisdom will manifest.

With wisdom, our minds can illuminate the true nature of all dharmas.

> *When not a single thought arises,*
> *the entire substance manifests.*

When the mind is completely stilled so that not a single shred of false thinking remains, we will be able to enter samadhi and our original wisdom will thus manifest. We will then truly understand the basic reason why we are human beings, and will no longer be moved by external things. When the myriad external conditions do not move our minds, we can then be considered to be:

> *In unmoving suchness where all is*
> *Absolutely clear and constantly understood.*

At that time, none of the eight winds: praise and ridicule, sorrow and joy, gain and loss, defamation and eulogy, will be able to move our minds.

> *People may praise us or ridicule us as they wish.*
> *In favorable or adverse conditions,*
> *We will advance vigorously.*
> *No suffering or joy will move our minds.*

Gain refers to things that benefit one, loss refers to things that harm one; defamation means to slander; eulogy is to commend or glorify one's name.

> *Unmoved by the eight winds,*
> *I sit erect on a purple-golden lotus.*

Not being blown about by the eight winds is the result of thought cultivation, of silencing the mind. By not being moved by external factors, we can then understand how to practice sitting meditation.

Silencing the mind reveals our wisdom.

Investigating Chan requires non-movement of the mind and thoughts and this means silence. The Chan method works like the thrust of a knife, cutting right through. Because Chan investigation is apart from the mind-consciousness, it is known as putting an end to the mind. Ending the mind means ending all mental activities of the mind-consciousness. Only when all the activities of the false mind are stopped will thoughts be silenced.

When that happens, we gain the power of knowing and seeing that comes with sudden enlightenment to the non-arising of all things. We then have patience with the non-arising of people and dharmas.

And we certify to four stages of practice, which are heat, summit, patience, and first in the world.

1. Heat. This warm energy comes as we sit in meditation.

2. Summit. That energy rises to the crown of our head as we continue to practice.

3. Patience. It becomes very difficult to be patient, but we must still be patient.

4. First in the World. We become a world-transcending great hero.

If we want to attain these four stages, we must first learn to silence the mind. Our mind-consciousness must remain unmoving.

Our thoughts are like waves that cannot be calmed. Sitting in meditation aims at stopping the mind-consciousness from moving. Eventually, it stops naturally. Once stopped, the mind is silent. When it is completely silent, wisdom comes forth. When wisdom arises, we become self-illuminating.

When silence reaches an ultimate point,
the light penetrates everywhere.

That is the power of knowing and seeing that comes with sudden enlightenment to the non-arising of all things.

The flavor of lightness and ease is infinitely wonderful.

What is the flavor of Chan? It is the joy of realizing Chan samadhi, which brings a feeling of lightness and tranquility. This infinitely wonderful experience defies conceptualization and verbal description. Those who have personally experienced this state tacitly accept it. Just as when a person drinks water, he himself will know whether it is hot or cold, so too lightness and ease is something we ourselves will know when it happens to us. If all of you want to know whether the flavor of Chan is sweet or bitter, you will have to work very hard at investigating Chan. When you have reached a certain state, you will naturally know the flavor.

Therefore, you have to investigate, and when you have investigated until the truth emerges, then you will experience the flavor of Chan. Chan is not to be spoken of but is to be investigated.

25

This is why the Chan sect does not teach using words or literature. Its truth is transmitted outside the Teaching. It is a method that points directly to the human mind so that one can see one's own nature and attain Buddhahood.

When a person who investigates Chan has reached a high level of attainment, he will never get angry. He will not fight or contend with others, because he has attained the Samadhi of Non-Contention. He will not pursue fame nor gain, because he looks upon wealth as being dewdrops on flowers. He looks upon official status as being frost on a rooftop. Both vanish without a trace in no time.

3. TEN BENEFITS OF CHAN

Ten benefits of Chan are gained from proper practice.

1. Adhering to practices that bring peaceful dwelling. When we sit in meditation and investigate Chan every day, we acquire a certain deportment. This deportment takes practice. When we investigate Chan year after year, month after month, day after day, hour after hour, and minute by minute, there are proper ways to practice.

Running meditation is one example. When it is time to do running meditation in the Chan hall, someone shouts, "Run!" Everyone runs. We may run until we perspire and almost pass out. We may run until we are not aware of the heavens above, the earth below, and people in between. During running meditation we can become unaware of our self, and fundamentally, there is no longer a self. When our running meditation reaches the point that we have no notion of self and others, we will be contemplating at ease. In the absence

28

of self, we will have no false thinking. In the absence of people, we will have no false thoughts of others. At that moment, we will be contemplating at ease.

> *Neither in emptiness nor in form*
> *Does one see the Thus Come One.*

The Buddha does not fall into the categories of emptiness or existence, which means he is neither empty nor does he have substance. Therefore, if we realize that the Dharma-body of the Thus Come One is neither empty nor has substance, then we have seen the Dharma-body of the Thus Come One. We arrive there by adhering to practices that bring peaceful dwelling.

2. Using kindness in what we do. This does not necessarily mean being nice to others. When it is necessary to use kindness, we should use kindness and compassion to teach and cross over the other person. We use the method of gathering in. If we encounter a sentient being who needs to be exhorted or admonished so that he can gain an awakening, we should be motivated by kindness and compassion as we exhort or admonish him.

Or, in the Chan Hall, the incense board is often used to tap people into an awakening. In the Chan Hall, there are often cases of people being hit. However, this kind of hitting is different from ordinary hitting for the intention here is to enable that person to be awakened. This is for his own good because we hope that he will observe the rules and get rid of his false thoughts. That is how to use kindness in what we do.

3. The absence of the heat of regret. The heat of regret is an affliction. In regretting, the mind indulges in affliction and that generates heat. Therefore, this third benefit means to be without afflictions.

4. Safeguarding the sense faculties. This means watching over the six sense faculties. Why do we need to safeguard the six faculties? If we do not, they will run away. The eyes will be drawn to forms; the ears will be enticed by sounds; the nose will react to smells; the tongue will get involved in tastes; the body will be influenced by touch; and the mind will indulge in mental constructs. That is why we have to safeguard the six faculties until they emit light and cause the earth to quake. Why do they emit light? Light is emitted when we have no more false thoughts and our original wisdom manifests. When the light of wisdom shines throughout the trichiliocosm, the six sense faculties emit light and the earth quakes.

5. Knowing the joy of non-eating. A person who investigates Chan will obtain the joy of Chan as food and be filled with Dharma joy. When that happens, then even though we do not eat substantial food, we will be joyful. Despite not consuming any food, we are happy so long as we can investigate Chan. Has this happened to any of you?

6. Being apart from emotional love and desire. When our minds do not entertain thoughts of emotional love and desire, then our minds are clear and

pure. Emotional love and desire are defilements and defilements result in birth and death. Why do ordinary human beings like us experience birth and death? It is because we have not cut off emotional love and desire.

Why do ordinary people keep revolving continuously in the six paths of rebirth without ever ending birth and death? It is because they entertain thoughts of emotional love and desire and can never stop doing so. If you cannot cut off love and desire, you cannot end birth and death. As long as we have not ended birth and death, we will revolve continuously in the six paths. If people who investigate Chan can be apart from thoughts of emotional love and desire, then the doors of hell will remain closed and they will not go there.

7. Cultivating will not be done in vain. What does that mean? It means the only thing to fear is that we will fail to cultivate. If we do cultivate, we will not pass the time in vain. When we sit in meditation for an hour, our wisdom-life will lengthen by an hour. When we meditate for two hours, our wisdom-life will extend by two hours. If we investigate Chan every moment, every hour, every day, every month and every year, our inherent wisdom will certainly become evident. Hence, Chan cultivation will never be done in vain. For as long as we cultivate, we will not pass the time in vain.

8. Remaining free of demonic karma. Cultivators can keep clear of the karmic power of demons. When

we are free from the karmic obstructions of demons, no demon can disturb or hinder us in any way.

9. Dwelling peacefully in the Buddha's realm. If we can investigate Chan constantly, we will gain this ninth benefit of dwelling peacefully in the Buddha's realm.

10. Gaining complete liberation. This is the benefit that everyone hopes for. Complete liberation means to be without obstructions. Having no obstructions, we realize the clear and pure Dharma-body.

These are the ten benefits of investigating Chan.

4. How to Investigate Chan.

a) Sitting Meditation

The vajra posture quells demons.

When sitting in Chan, make sure your posture is correct. A correct posture benefits both body and mind. Without it, sitting in Chan loses its meaning. When we sit in meditation, we need to first relax the body and mind. Do not become tense. It would be ideal to sit in full lotus, which is the basic posture. To sit in full lotus, first put the left foot over the right thigh, and then move the right foot over the left leg. This is also called the vajra position, which means it is firm and unmoving. All the Buddhas of the past attained Buddhahood by sitting in the vajra position. In this sitting posture, we can subdue demons from the heavens and counter those of externalist ways. When they see us in this position, they surrender and retreat, not daring to come forward and create trouble.

Once we are sitting in the full-lotus posture, our eyes should contemplate the tip of our nose and not look left and right.

The eyes contemplate the nose.
The nose contemplates the mouth.
The mouth contemplates the heart.

This way, we can gather in our body and mind. The mind is like a monkey or a wild horse, and you must tie it up so it does not run away. It is said,

Concentration brings,
Results that are efficacious.
Being scattered,
Results in nothing at all.

We need to sit properly, keeping our back straight and our head up. Do not lean forward, backward, or to the left or right. Sit firmly, being as stable as a large bell, the kind that does not sway or move. Do not be like a small bell's clapper that swings back and forth. Full lotus is the proper posture for sitting in Chan. Beginners in Chan meditation who are not used to it may experience pain in their legs and may get a backache. Do not worry. Just grit your teeth and be patient for a while, and those sensations will naturally subside. The saying goes, "With long sitting, there is Chan." So, keep at it and you will naturally attain the flavor of Chan.

Full-lotus posture makes it easy to enter samadhi.

Full-lotus posture is another name for the vajra posture just described. By placing our left foot on top of our right thigh and then placing our right foot on our left thigh, we achieve full-lotus position. The left foot belongs to yang while the right foot belongs to yin. When assuming this meditation posture, the left foot, which is yang, is placed first, so that it is under, while the right foot, which is yin, is placed second on top.

This balance of yin and yang can be seen in the taiji symbol, which depicts the absolute, from which comes primal beginning, and then from primal beginning, the two primary forces of yin and yang are shown symbolically as intertwined fish.

For those who prefer, it is also acceptable to put the left foot below and the right foot on top. The

Dharma is not fixed and can be adapted according to a person's preference. It is not necessary to attach rigidly to the particulars of the sitting posture. I am teaching the classic method, where the left foot goes on the right thigh and the right foot on the left thigh. It is not a fixed rule that you have to sit in this position.

In conclusion, lotus posture facilitates entry into samadhi. It makes it much easier to do so. If we could enter samadhi while walking, it would not be necessary to sit. The state of samadhi is devoid of false thoughts. When the mind does not entertain a single thought, then it will not be defiled by even a single speck of dust. When our mind entertains no thoughts and is not defiled by even a speck of dust, then we can continue to develop our skill while walking, standing, sitting, and reclining. At that point, we will not be limited to the sitting posture alone.

Once your legs no longer ache, you have really begun investigating Chan.

When you first learn how to sit in full lotus posture, if your legs feel stiff and painful, you may sit in a more comfortable manner. Thereafter, you should learn to sit in half lotus position. Then when your legs do not feel so painful, you can learn to sit in full lotus position. When your legs no longer ache, you have really begun investigating Chan. That marks the actual beginning.

Basically, Chan investigation is intentionally looking for something to do when one has nothing to do. For instance, a cultivator who has eaten his fill, slept enough, is warmly clothed and has nothing else to do, will then investigate Chan. Getting good at it, we can then roam and play in the world.

Sit straight without leaning.

The basic posture of sitting meditation requires us to hold our body upright. We must sit straight and not allow ourselves to lean this way or that. However, you should not force yourself. It must come naturally. Turn the tip of your tongue back and let the underside of your tongue touch the roof of your mouth. Then swallow your saliva. When it flows into your stomach, it can balance your energy and blood.

Sweet dew cures many illnesses.

When sitting in Chan with our tongue rolled back so its underside touches the roof of our mouth, we may generate a lot of saliva. We should swallow it. That saliva is called sweet dew. Why? After we practice Chan sitting for an extended period of time, our saliva becomes sweet. Although it may not be as sweet and thick as sugar or honey, it still has a faint sweetness. When we regularly swallow that sweet dew, we will not feel hungry or thirsty, even without food or drink.

When a person's practice reaches the stage where he is not aware of walking, standing, sitting or reclining, his skill merges with every movement, and he is in samadhi in every instant. This is described thus:

> *The Naga remains in stillness always,*
> *There is never a moment of non-stillness.*

The sweet dew we swallow can cure numerous illnesses, strengthen us physically, and help us open our wisdom. But we must practice diligently without interruption. Why is it that cultivators do not wish to talk much? They need to concentrate on their practice. No matter what they are doing, be it gathering firewood, fetching water, welcoming guests and seeing them off, or traveling about, they are always practicing hard. When our skill reaches maturity, then even without any volitional effort, we will still continue to practice hard. Even without volitional effort, we will be investigating "Who is mindful of the Buddha?" When we investigate to the point that we are not moved by wind or rain, our skill will become such that wind and rain cannot encroach upon us. Of course, this sort of skill is not accomplished overnight. That is why, at all times, we have to be mindful of the present.

Sweet dew is also referred to as "our own drink" and is recognized as a medicine. It is an elixir that enhances longevity. It is a medicine that brings liberation from birth and death. It is a tonic for escaping the cycle of rebirth in the six realms of existence. Everyone has this medicine but most refuse to take it. Most people ignore the root and are attracted by branch tips. In other words, they search high and low outside.

This sweet-dew tonic originates from our self-nature. If we constantly apply effort in our practice, our saliva becomes sweet, even sweeter than honey. When that medicine takes effect, the body will undergo changes internally. Those who have not experienced this benefit in cultivation do not know what I am talking about. Those who have experienced it will be ever-diligent. They will not put off cultivation or take breaks. We must be persistent in our practice and constantly guard it. Practice should not be erratic, such that we:

> Fish for three days,
> and then dry the net for two.
> Heat something for one day,
> and then let it get cold for ten.
> Pluck a lotus blossom today,
> and then pick a peony tomorrow.

We need firm sincerity and honest determination. We must constantly practice hard in order to progress on the Path. To progress one day and then retreat the next is a waste of time.

Eyes contemplate nose.
Nose contemplates mouth.
Mouth contemplates heart.

When sitting in meditation, sit up straight and erect. Do not lean backwards or forwards and do not lower your head. Keep the head upright. The eyes should look at the nose to see if the nostrils are pointing upwards or downwards. Pay close attention to it. The nose should watch the mouth. But, you wonder, does the nose have eyes? By focusing on the mouth, the nose will gradually develop eyes. The more you focus the nose on the mouth, the sooner the nose will actually see the mouth. The nose contemplates the mouth, and the mouth inquires of the heart. Inquire into whether your own heart is black, white, yellow or red. What kind of heart is it? Go ahead and inquire into that.

If you discover that it is black, then you have to turn the black heart into a white one. When you see your black heart turning white day-by-day until it becomes a treasury of brilliant light that integrates with the Dharma Realm, then you can know you are gaining a little skill. Do not breathe through your mouth. Breathe through your nose. Sometimes the nasal passages are blocked which makes breathing through the nose difficult. However, if you can breathe through your nose, when you inhale, bring the breath down to just behind the navel, not below it. That place is empty and is without anything. In fact, from the beginning there has never been anything there. That is the place where your breath has to stop.

Sometimes people who practice will ask, "Do you know how to catch your breath?" That is a very important question. If you can catch your breath, then your external breathing becomes an internal breathing. That internal breathing replaces the external breathing. This is why a practitioner with sufficient skill does not breathe externally. That external breathing has stopped, but the internal breathing functions. With internal breathing there is no exhalation through the nose or mouth, but all the pores on the body are breathing. A person who is breathing internally appears to be dead, but actually he has not died. He does not breathe externally, but the internal breathing comes alive.

At that time, when your eyes see forms, inside there is nothing, because all forms have been emptied. The ears hear sounds but the mind does not know. When you contemplate your mind, the mind is also empty. Looking out for forms, forms vanish; looking afar at objects, they too become empty. But at this point, you should not think that you are great. You have merely activated an initial expedient and are experiencing the state of lightness and ease. Do not mistake a thief for your own son. Do not mistake where you are in your practice, thinking that you are already very great.

Heat, Summit, Patience, First in the World.

When sitting in meditation, the underside of the tongue touches the roof of the mouth. This is the point where the two channels of *ren* and *du* connect. When these two channels are clear, then the circulation of energy and blood is also clear, and one feels at ease. When there is saliva in the mouth, swallow it into the stomach. Doing this frequently is just like using sweet dew to water and nourish a young Bodhi sprout. After sitting for some time, a warm energy fills the body and it may become very hot. At this stage, certain changes begin to occur.

1. Heat is the first stage. This warmth originates at the cinnabar, the point just behind the navel, spreads to the whole body, and then circulates back to the cinnabar. This warm energy circulates like that again and again during the stage of heat.

2. Summit is the second stage. When you have

experienced the warmth for some time, during which your body's chemical plant has done the necessary experiments, you will then reach the summit. At the summit, you feel as if there is something at the top of your head, yet there appears to be nothing there. If you say there is something, you cannot see it or touch it. You only experience this feeling at the top of your head, and you will invariably feel it is indescribable.

3. Patience is the third stage. After the summit stage, you begin to experience an unbearable feeling. No matter how unbearable this feeling is, you have to endure it. This is known as the stage of patience. After the summit stage comes the stage of patience. It is very difficult to pass the stage of patience because of the discomfort associated with the top of your head. It seems as if there is something trying to drill a hole through to the outside. At this point, you have to be very patient. As time goes by, the drill penetrates through and emerges from the top of your head, just like a little bird that has been set free from its cage. And like a freed bird, you will feel exceptionally happy.

4. First in the World is the fourth stage. Getting free is called being foremost in the world. This can refer to having the world's foremost patience. It is also known as being the World's Number One Great Personage, or the World's Number One Great Hero. Being peerless, you are known as Number One in the World. Even so, you will still have to be careful and continue to cultivate every day.

Subduing guest-dust afflictions is like letting muddy water settles.

When we sit in Chan, we have to cleanse our mind and reduce our desires. This is the first step in cultivation. Cleansing the mind refers to subduing afflictions, which are transient, like a guest who does not stay, like particles of dust that fly about. Our turbid afflictions make us like a jar of muddy water. If we keep shaking the jar, the water will remain murky and we will not be able to see the bottom of the jar clearly. But if, after we pour the muddy water into a jar, we do not disturb the jar, then the mud and silt will settle to the bottom.

This is the first step in subduing guest-dust afflictions. Sitting properly in meditation for even one *ksana* (a moment) generates more merit than building as many pagodas of the seven jewels as there are sand grains in the Ganges River. That is because by sitting in meditation, we can subdue our guest-dust afflictions and allow the silt of the five desires to settle down.

> *A clear mind is as a still pool*
> *that can reflect the moon.*
> *A calm will is as a bright sky*
> *without a trace of clouds.*

Investigate Chan while walking, standing, sitting and reclining.

Chan sitting cannot be considered fun. It involves enduring a lot of hardship. We begin our first sit at three o'clock in the morning and we continue sitting and walking right up to twelve o'clock midnight. Our rest period at night is only three hours long. In the afternoon there is also a one-hour optional rest period. During Chan investigation, we have to forget about the body, the mind, the world, and everything else. Even the self must no longer exist. Everything becomes empty. When we reach the state of true emptiness, wonderful existence will appear. Everybody must pay attention to this! During cultivation, do not talk unnecessarily. Try not to have false thoughts. Take care not to be lazy or stop to rest. We should treasure every minute and every second. As it is said,

A moment passed is a moment less of life.

Therefore, we have to investigate Chan while walking, standing, sitting, and reclining. Cultivating Chan at all times, we have to constantly pay attention to our investigation. The more we investigate, the more transparent and bright we become.

Concentrate. Persevere.

When we investigate Chan, we should not fear backaches and pain in our legs. We must draw on our *vajra* will and use patience and perseverance to investigate Chan. We must constantly persevere and be firm and uncompromising in our resolve. In every moment, we must practice hard. In the past, virtuous elders in the monastic Sangha, having practiced sitting meditation for many years, continued to sit. This shows that cultivation is not so simple and easy. We must endure. We cannot pluck a lotus blossom today and pick a peony tomorrow.

We should not think that by sitting for a day we can become enlightened. We need to understand the importance of patience when practicing Chan sitting.

How do we concentrate? Well, imagine the intensity with which a young girl pursues a boy she likes, or how a boy chases a girl. That is how concentrated we should be in meditation. If we can be that determined and intent on our investigation of Chan, so that we are ever-mindful of the present, then there is no reason why we cannot succeed.

Sit solidly, like a big bell.
Walk gently, like a light breeze.

By investigating Chan, we cultivate samadhi. Chan investigation is neither conditional nor unconditional. Superficially, Chan investigation appears to be unconditional. Actually, when we investigate Chan, we are helping to increase the proper energy in the Dharma Realm. If everyone investigated Chan, there would be no wars in this world. It is said that:

Sitting for a long time, we will gain Chan.

But Chan investigation is not only done while sitting. We can investigate Chan while standing, walking, or reclining as well.

A hardworking cultivator does not allow mundane matters to bother him. He holds the meditation topic at every moment. Remaining ever in the present, we investigate, "Who is mindful of the Buddha?" When, through our investigation, the mountains disappear and the waters vanish, then in that ultimate state, we will naturally exhibit awesome deportment in our walking, standing, sitting, and reclining.

1. Sit like a bell. Sit solidly. Do not be like a pendulum that swings to and fro. Sit erect and upright, with the eyes contemplating the nose, the nose contemplating the mouth and the mouth contemplating the heart. With the underside of your tongue touching the roof of your mouth, you swallow the saliva as it is secreted.

2. Walk like a breeze. During the short running period, run like the wind. Let that wind blow to the point that the heavens above disappear, the very earth dissolves, and all people in between are gone. When one is working hard, there is no mark of others and therefore, there is no heaven above, no earth below and no people in between. During the longer walking periods, we should walk like a breeze without causing any ripples.

3. Stand like an evergreen. While standing, keep your back straight. Stand upright, just like a lofty evergreen tree.

4. Recline like a bow. When lying down, assume the auspicious reclining posture. Lie on your right side with your right hand under your right cheek and your left hand resting along your left side. The Great Master Yong Jia said,

Walking is Chan, sitting is Chan.
In speech or silence, in movement or stillness,
My body is at ease.
Even if someone drew a knife on me,
I would remain calm.
Even if someone poisoned me,
I would not get upset.

Master Bodhidharma, the first patriarch in China, was poisoned on six occasions by externalists. Even though he knew very well that it was poison, he still consumed it. Thus, we know that he was devoid of self and could look lightly on birth and death.

When cultivators work hard, the heavens shake and the earth quakes, and ghosts and spirits weep. Even the demon kings are shocked. By working hard in our practice, we can keep the demon kings from being able to exert their power. That shocks them. If we could practice diligently for these twenty-one hours-a-day and work hard every second, we would surely cause the heavens to shake and the earth to quake.

In practicing to reach unconditional dharmas, we begin with conditional dharmas. We should not be afraid of the toil of the running periods and the sitting periods. Running can be likened to the conditional while sitting can be likened to the unconditional. Hence, the saying,

Within the unconditioned are conditions.
Within conditions lies the unconditioned.
What is conditional is also unconditional.
The conditioned is unconditioned.
The unconditioned is conditioned.

As skill increases, afflictions decrease.

Sitting in Chan is like being a horse trainer or a monkey trainer. It is not easy. Although it is not easy, we still have to sit regardless of how difficult it is. In this world, whatever you want to do is not easy and requires a lot of effort.

Chan sitting is also like that. It requires a good deal of hard work and effort. If we could restrain our mad mind and calm our wild nature, and if we could confine ignorance and false thoughts to a single location, then our skill would increase day-by-day and our afflictions would decrease correspondingly.

Sitting in meditation is like unraveling a silken cocoon.

When we sit in meditation, we are as if unraveling the silk from a cocoon. We are like silkworms encased in a cocoon, caught in the six desires and bound by the seven emotions, which are joy, anger, sorrow, fear, emotional love, hatred, and desire. Although these seven emotions cannot be eradicated immediately, they should be reduced bit-by-bit.

1. Joy. We should not be excessively happy to the point of laughing as if we had gone mad.

2. Anger. Furthermore, we should not display anger. As it is said,

> *The fire of ignorance, blazing like the stars,*
> *will consume a forest of merit and virtue.*
> *Firewood collected over a thousand days*
> *can be burned up by a single spark.*

If your mind is calm when you sit in Chan, then you

59

will feel very peaceful. However, if you indulge in anger, you will be afflicted with a hundred types of illnesses. The bones and joints in your whole body will be very painful. The fire of anger will have burned down the Bodhi tree.

3. Sorrow. We should not allow ourselves to become overly sad.

4. Fear. With fear in the mind, we cannot achieve righteousness.

5. Emotional love. Suppose we see someone or something beautiful and react with craving and desire. Suppose we notice that others have nice things and we crave such things ourselves. Such craving comes from thoughts that are caught up in emotional love and greed.

6. Hatred. Hatred is the opposite of emotional love. Extreme love often turns into hatred.

7. Desire. This includes thoughts of desire, and especially those that are unruly, not in accord with the Way.

These seven emotions have to be eradicated bit-by-bit. Hence, in our practice, it is necessary to continually cleanse our mind. When the seven emotions have been reduced to the point of disappearing, then there will be nothing left. At that point, we will be constantly in samadhi. Whether we are walking, standing, sitting, or reclining, we will be investigating Chan and practicing hard. It is then that we will recognize our original face and know whether our nostrils are pointing up or down.

Sit perfectly still.

Sitting perfectly still for even an instant,
Generates more merit than
Building pagodas of the seven gems
In number like the Ganges' sands.

An instant includes numberless great kalpas. Numberless big kalpas are not beyond the present thought. The present thought does not go beyond numberless great kalpas. If we could sit perfectly still for even a split second, then there would be no mark of people, self, others, and a lifespan. Not a single thought would arise and all conditions would cease. At that point in time, one compresses numberless great kalpas into a single thought, and one expands a single thought to include numberless great kalpas. But even if we can sit still for a split second, or half an hour, or for three hours or five hours, or even for seven days and nights, we still have to keep on sitting. Then, we come to realize that inside there is no body and mind, and outside there is no world. This kind of merit and virtue is greater than that of building seven-jeweled pagodas numbering like Ganges' sands.

Why is that so? It is because the merit and virtue of building pagodas have form and will cease to exist eventually. If you can reach the state of having no mark of body and mind, and no mark of the world, then at that moment, your own *prajna* wisdom will emerge. This type of wisdom is such that one looks but does not see, hears but does not listen, and smells but takes in no scent. Nevertheless, one's enlightened awareness remains.

If we could, in an instant, or in a very short span of time, have no mark of others, no mark of self, no mark of living beings, and no mark of a lifespan, then we would be in accord with our inherent Buddha nature. The inherent Buddha nature can illuminate the true nature of all Dharmas. It does not come into being or cease to be. It is not defiled and not pure. It neither increases nor diminishes. The sunshine of our inherent wisdom cannot shine through because we are covered by ignorance. The dark clouds of ignorance plunge us into obscurity. As a result, we are unable to discern right from wrong and vice versa. We recognize a thief for a son and are always engaged in upside-down false thinking. This is why we keep roaming about in birth and death, unable to extricate ourselves from it.

4. HOW TO INVESTIGATE CHAN

b) THE MEDITATION TOPIC

Fighting poison with poison,
a false thought stops false thoughts.

When investigating Chan, we use a meditation topic, an inquiry into what precedes the state of no thought. The most common meditation topic is "Who is mindful of the Buddha?" The inquiry into "who?" is sustained, just as though we were using a drill to pierce a hole through the mind. When we find out "who", then we will be enlightened. However, we cannot deduce this by using our imagination. We cannot investigate it with our mind consciousness. Instead, we have to explore and search for where we have never been and what we have never known. Sometimes a breakthrough in the investigation brings sudden enlightenment. Space is shattered and the five skandhas disintegrate.

This is described in the *Heart Sutra*:

When Bodhisattva Avalokiteshvara was practicing the profound prajna paramita, he illuminated the five skandas

and saw that they are all empty, and he crossed beyond all suffering and difficulty. Shariputra! Form does not differ from emptiness; emptiness does not differ from form. Form itself is emptiness; emptiness itself is form. So too are all feeling, cognition, formation, and consciousness.

When our investigation leads to the disintegration of the five skandhas, then we will not be influenced by the six sense objects. That is the first step to accomplishing Buddhahood.

However, we still have to work very hard. Furthermore, you should know that Chan investigation is different from vigorously chanting the Buddha's name. We do not incessantly chant, "Who is mindful of the Buddha? Who is mindful of the Buddha? Who is mindful of the Buddha," as if we were shouting for help. Investigating the meditation topic has to be done slowly, as we carefully search for our self-nature. As it is said,

> *Investigating brings awakening.*
> *Awakening requires investigating.*

Actually, "Who is mindful of the Buddha?" is also a false thought, but it is a case of using poison to fight poison. We use one false thought to stop all false thoughts.

Go with care.
Avoid demonic possession.

The meditation topic we investigate is one false thought. Our mind is full of many scattered thoughts. By using the method of fighting poison with poison, we use one false thought to stop all our many false thoughts. Slowly, one by one, we eradicate false thoughts, so they no longer have influence on us. At that time, no matter what state arises, we will not be deluded by it. We will distinguish things clearly and not become possessed by demons. The ancients said,

> *It would be better to go without enlightenment*
> *for a thousand lifetimes, than to be possessed by a*
> *demon for even a single day.*

As we cultivate Chan meditation, we must be cautious and circumspect, and not get carried away. We must be proper, magnanimous, and forthright, so that demons have no chance to trouble us. Idle thoughts open the door to demons, but the meditation topic is the Dharma-treasure that exorcises those demons.

Concentrate on a single meditation topic.

In Chan meditation, we can investigate a few meditation topics such as "Who is mindful of the Buddha?" or "What was my original face before my parents gave birth to me?" or "What is it that we cannot do without?" If all of you can investigate single-mindedly, you will definitely obtain benefits.

Let not a single thought arise.
Be mindful of the present.

Investigation is similar to drilling wood; you do not stop until the drill makes a hole all the way through the wood. If you stop halfway, then all your earlier efforts will be to no avail. The first priority in Chan meditation is patience. When you can be entirely patient, then you can reach a state of "not even one thought arising". When not even one thought arises, you can get enlightened. As the saying goes, *Take one more step from the very top of a hundred-foot pole.* At that time, when you can take yet another step from the very top of a hundred-foot pole, *the worlds throughout the ten directions manifest in their entirety.* To gain success, however, you must apply yourself constantly, in thought after thought, without any laziness or slacking off.

Be as a cat is when stalking a mouse. Be as a dragon is when guarding its pearl.

Investigating Chan is just like using a drill to create a hole. You must keep on drilling until you have broken through. Drilling through is known as "breaking the fundamental investigation". Having drilled a hole through, brightness will be revealed. In this dark house, without any windows and doors, you have to use a drill to make a hole. When a hole has been made, light will shine in. When you are still ignorant and do not understand anything, it is just like being in a dark room without windows and doors. If, in using this skill to investigate Chan, you succeed in drilling through, light will shine in. This is investigating Chan.

There is another analogy. Meditation is just like *a cat stalking a mouse*. When a cat stalks a mouse, it watches the mouse-hole intently. The moment the mouse comes out, the cat pounces on it and grabs it with its paw. The mouse has no way of escaping. What is the 'mouse'? It represents your ignorance. When you emit light, it is similar to a cat that has caught the mouse.

Yet there is another analogy. It is like *a dragon nurturing its pearl*. A dragon never strays from his gem. When two dragons fight over a pearl, they treat it as even more precious than their own lives. Hence, a dragon will think of ways and means to protect its pearl. In the same way, a Chan investigator is like a dragon that nurtures its pearl constantly in thought after thought. This is called contemplating at ease. If you can contemplate at ease, you are ever mindful of the present. However, if you cannot contemplate at ease, that means you are running away! What happens when you run away? It means you give in to false thoughts. As soon as you have false thoughts, you will not be at ease. When you do not have false thoughts, then you are at ease.

Let me give you another example. What is meditation like? It is like *a hen brooding over her eggs*. When the hen broods over her eggs, she thinks, "I am here sitting on the eggs. When the time comes, the chicks will hatch. Little chicks will definitely appear". When you investigate Chan, it is similar to a hen brooding over her eggs. You reflect, "Oh! One day I will be enlightened. When I practice for one day, my self-nature will shine forth a bit of light. If I practice every day, then my wisdom light will shine forth constantly. Eventually, I will want to be the same as the Buddha, not in the least bit different." When you investigate in this way, you are just like the hen brooding over her eggs, and one day you will succeed! This is Chan investigation.

Our meditation topic works like the Headband-tightening Mantra.

When we sit in meditation, we have to catch the little monkey. The human mind is like a wild horse. Our thoughts are as restless and naughty as a monkey. If we do not catch that monkey, it will just keep giving us the runaround. Our essence and spirit will be scattered and our energy source will become depleted to exhaustion. The energy source of the self-nature is very precious. If it is depleted by the monkey for no rhyme or reason, then it is really not worth it. Now, we need to train the horse to obey instructions and tame the monkey so that it will be obedient. This means you have to tame the wild-horse mind and monkey-like thoughts. How do you do it? You need to tie on a golden headband and then chant the Headband-tightening Mantra. In the novel Journey to the West, as soon as Xuan Zhuang, the Tang monk, chanted the Headband-tightening Mantra, the monkey-god, Sun Wu Kong, became very obedient.

75

What is our Headband-tightening Mantra? The inquiry into 'who' in our meditation topic "Who is mindful of the Buddha?" will work. Use it and the monkeylike thoughts will become obedient. Since the monkey in our mind does not know who that 'who' is, it will concentrate single-mindedly to search for it. Once our monkeylike thoughts quiet down, our mind will attentively concentrate in its search and our thoughts will no longer give us the runaround. If you can catch the monkey and tame it, then your skill is almost there!

If you are apart from this, you have gone amiss.

Investigating Chan goes beyond the hard work we do while sitting in meditation. We have to work hard while walking, standing, sitting, or reclining. Sitting meditation provides the opportunity to concentrate on the focal point of our meditation topic. Then, while walking, standing, sitting, and reclining, we continue to investigate "Who is mindful of the Buddha?"

The entire verse reads,

> *Walking, standing, sitting, and lying down,*
> *Do not be apart from this.*
> *If you are apart from this,*
> *You have gone amiss.*

What is *this*? It refers to our investigation of our meditation topic, "Who is mindful of the Buddha?"

Sweep away all dharmas.
Separate from all marks.

Those who do not understand the method of Chan investigation may treat it like chanting the Buddha's name, thinking that the more you chant the better it is. That would be a mistake. Inquiry into the meditation topic is not done by chanting it. The best way is to stretch the resonance of the inquiry so that it lasts for a few hours without ending. That inquiry could even continue for eighty-thousand great kalpas without interruption. That would truly be investigating Chan.

Why do we investigate "Who is mindful of the Buddha?" The word "who" is basically superfluous, but we are like monkeys, always looking around for something to do. With the word "who" acting as a shield, we can deflect all those idle thoughts. This Dharma-door uses poison to fight poison. Only when we are free of all random thoughts can we be said to be diligently wiping the mirror of our mind clean at all times. To investigate Chan simply means to diligently wipe the mirror of the mind clean. Why must we keep wiping it clean? We must do that to keep the mind from attracting dust. This is the Dharma-door of "sweeping away all dharmas, and separating from all marks."

If you do not use Dharma-selecting vision so that you recognize true Dharma, then you do not really know how to investigate. If you do not learn how to investigate, your efforts will just be wasted. That is because if you fail to recognize proper Dharma, you may well end up following deviant dharmas. That is why Dharma-selecting vision is so important.

Contemplate at ease to find wisdom.

Investigating Chan means learning to contemplate. What are we to contemplate? Contemplate your illuminating prajna. I am teaching you to be mindful of the present and to contemplate yourself, not to contemplate others. Contemplate whether you are here or not? If you are here, then you can sit and investigate Chan, working hard at cultivation. If you are not here, then you are indulging in false thinking and are daydreaming. Even though you are physically in the Chan hall, your mind has gone to New York sightseeing, or to Italy for a holiday. Your mind goes everywhere, climbing on conditions. Hence, you are not at ease.

To contemplate at ease is to be a Bodhisattva. Not contemplating at ease, you are an ordinary person. To contemplate at ease is to experience the divine. If you do not contemplate at ease, you may end up enduring the hells. If you contemplate at ease and your mind does not escape, then you can practice profound prajna paramita. By physically investigating Chan continuously without cease, you are also practicing profound prajna, and discovering your wisdom. Once you activate your inherent great wisdom, then you can reach the other shore.

The secret to Chan investigation is to focus on it day and night. Focus on what? "Who is mindful of the Buddha?" Investigate this today and again tomorrow. Even though you practice profound prajna paramita in the Chan hall everyday, you may not taste the flavor of Chan right away. It takes a long time to accomplish that. Only when you have gained sufficient skill in practicing profound prajna paramita will you be able to illuminate the five skandhas and see that they are all empty.

When we gain the One, all things are done.

The secret of investigating Chan is to gain one-pointed focus. As the saying goes,

> *When Heaven attains the One,*
> *it becomes pure;*
> *When Earth attains the One,*
> *it becomes peaceful;*
> *When a person attains the One,*
> *he becomes a sage.*
> *When all things attain the One,*
> *they all abide in their destiny.*

This is why the One is the beginning of all things. However, it is still not the ultimate Dharma. It is said,

> *When you obtain the One,*
> *all things are done.*

But if you are attach to the One, then you will fall into two or three, and that is not true emptiness. What is true

82

emptiness? It is Zero. The Zero is formed by making a circle. It is neither big nor small, neither inside nor outside, has no beginning and no end and cannot be enumerated. However, all numbers are not apart from it. Cultivation starts with cultivating the One until you return to Zero. From Zero, uncountable functions come forth. Although it is said that 'when you obtain the One, all things are done', at the stage of Zero, there is not a single thing. At that point,

> *When not one Dharma is established,*
> *the myriad conditions are empty.*

That is the ultimate liberation!

5. THE STATES OF CHAN

The States of the Four Dhyanas

The process of investigating Chan is similar to studying. You go from primary school to secondary school, to college and then to a research institute. After passing these four stages, you can then obtain a doctorate. The Dharma-door of Chan investigation is also like that. It is divided into four steps, that is, the four states of Chan. These are briefly described below:

1. The First Dhyana.

The State of Happiness That Leaves Beings Behind.

This means that we depart from our relationship with all beings and obtain another type of happiness. This happiness is different from that of ordinary beings. It emanates from within the skill of our self-nature. When we reach the state of the First Dhyana, our breathing stops. The external breathing stops, while the internal breathing comes alive. This phenomenon

85

is like what happens during winter hibernation. It defies description. At that time, our mind is as clear as water and as bright as a mirror. It illuminates the fundamental substance of our self-nature, even as we are aware that we are sitting in meditation.

2. The Second Dhyana.

The State of Happiness that comes with Samadhi.

In samadhi, we experience happiness beyond compare. This has come to be known as,

> *The joy of Chan being as food,*
> *The bliss of Dharma filling us up.*

When we experience such happiness, we will not feel hungry. That is why people can go without food or drink for many days and still be all right. But we cannot be attached to this state. If we become attached, all our efforts will be wasted. It is even possible to enter a demonic state because of attachment. We must be very cautious. At the stage of the Second Dhyana, not only does our breathing stop, but our pulse stops as well. When we leave this state of concentration, our pulse returns to normal.

3. The Third Dhyana.

The State of Exquisite Bliss that Comes with Transcending Happiness.

Here, we leave the happiness of the Second Dhyana and reach a level of exquisite and subtle bliss. We will

86

feel that everything is the Buddhadharma and that all things are blissful. In this stage of the Third Dhyana, when we enter the state of concentration, not only do our breathing and pulse stop, but our thoughts also stop. At that time, we have no thought of good or bad and no thought of right or wrong. In short, we have no more idle thoughts at all. However, we must not think that we are very special, for this is just part of a process. We are still a long way from ending birth and death.

4. The Fourth Dhyana.

The State of Purity of Dispensing with Thought Entirely.

At this stage, even the thought of happiness is gone, as we have already discarded it. We have reached the pure state of nothing whatsoever, in which things are neither conditioned nor unconditioned. The Fourth Dhyana is a stage that we who investigate Chan must experience. There is nothing special about this. We should not make the mistake of assuming that we have achieved the fruition of the Way. If we think like that, then we are making the same mistake as the unlearned bhiksu and will fall into the hells.

The state of the Fourth Dhyana is still at the stage of a common mortal. If we make vigorous progress, we will certify to states that enable us to enter the Five Heavens of No Return. Only then will we have actually reached the level of a certified sage. However, even at that stage, we will have still not ended birth and death. We have to transcend the Triple Realm in order to end the cycle of birth and death. You have to be clear on this point and not be confused.

An Arhat of the First Fruition is free of idle thoughts, not only when in samadhi, but also when walking, standing, sitting, and reclining. At the First Fruition, they have ended attachments, but they must still pass through seven more births and deaths.

Do not assume that the First Fruition brings one to Nirvana. Those sages have merely cut through eighty-eight levels of Delusions of Views in the Triple Realm. The minds of Arhats of the First Fruition are not swayed, no matter what sight meets their eyes. They do not indulge in superfluous thoughts when facing situations. They have only the thought of the Way as they cultivate Chan single-mindedly. Even if very attractive states appear to them, such as a lovely woman or a handsome man, their minds will not be moved. At this level, they experience no greed for wealth, sex, fame, food, or sleep.

They are indifferent to all of these desires. Only those who reach this level of skill can be called, "One who has realized the fruition". An Arhat of the First Fruition makes no sound with his feet when he walks. His feet are an inch or so above the earth. Why? People who have attained the fruition are possessed of kindness and compassion. They are extremely concerned about not harming small insects as they walk, so they prefer to travel in the air.

Merging with the great void, we have a sudden breakthrough.

Here in the Chan Hall, we should work at our cultivation to the point that we are unaware of the heavens above, people in between, and the earth below. If heaven, earth, and people have all disappeared, and north, south, east, and west are forgotten, then right at that point, when not even a single thought comes forth, the entire substance can manifest. Then, we will obtain the great functioning of the entire substance. However, if we indulge in idle thoughts all day long, there will certainly be no response to our efforts. Thus, we have to work to the point where not a single thought arises, and when we walk, we are not aware that we are walking. When we stand, we are not aware that we are standing. When we sit, we are unconscious of sitting. When we lie down, we are not conscious of lying down. We have no conscious awareness of walking, standing, sitting, and lying down. At that point,

We eat, but are not aware of
consuming a single grain of rice.
We dress, but are unaware of
putting on a single stitch.

The ego merges with space itself at that point. When we can unite with space, then we can have a sudden breakthrough and instantly understand all things. That is the state of sudden enlightenment.

Sudden enlightenment is a result of daily cultivation. When we get a response from our daily efforts, we can suddenly become enlightened. If we normally do not cultivate, then we will never gain sudden enlightenment. Similarly, after a child is born, he is steeped in words and sounds every day. When the time comes, he is naturally able to talk. When he utters his very first word, it is analogous to the enlightenment experience. Then when the time comes, he will naturally be able to walk, and that first step he takes is also like the enlightenment experience.

How can he take his first step? It is because he has been observing how adults walk every day. Being steeped in that environment, very naturally he will be able to walk. Cultivation works the same way. We cultivate today, we cultivate tomorrow, we cultivate on and on until our skills elicit a response. Then, when not a single thought is produced and our idle thoughts are dispelled, we will be enlightened.

This form of enlightenment may be due to cultivating diligently every day for every moment in this lifetime. When your skill matures, you will be enlightened. This enlightenment is due to diligent cultivation in this lifetime. At this point, someone might say, "I have seen a person who did not cultivate hard at all, and yet not long after coming to the Chan hall, he became enlightened. What is the reason?" That case is unique. Although the person did not cultivate hard in this lifetime, he had been cultivating hard in his previous lives. Not only did he cultivate, but also he had cultivated in each and every moment. However, he was just a little short of enlightenment. In this lifetime, when he encountered this state again, he became enlightened.

Although sudden enlightenment comes in a moment, it still depends on all the good roots one has carefully and continually nurtured in past lives. We are like a farmer planting a field. In the spring, he sows the seeds. In the summer, he weeds and hoes. Then in the autumn, there are crops to harvest. If he does not sow the seeds in spring, how can he reap the harvest when autumn comes? As the saying goes, "*One share of plowing and weeding done yields one share of harvest*". We cultivators of the Way are the same. Regardless of whether we are enlightened or not, we should still be courageous and vigorous in our cultivation. We should energetically stride forward. Then we have hope of gathering our harvest in the final moment and recognize our original face.

When sitting in meditation, do not seek for spiritual penetrations.

When sitting in meditation, do not seek for spiritual penetrations or for any efficacious result. First, make your body clean without any sicknesses. In this way, no deviant energy will be able to penetrate your boundary. If you are constantly filled with great proper energy and have an indomitable spirit, you will naturally give rise to proper knowledge and proper views. Your conduct and actions will accord with principle. This is the benefit of sitting in meditation.

If, in every instant, your state of mind does not give rise to ripples such that you are without afflictions, without mark of right and wrong, and without mark of people and self, then you are applying effort and this is the efficacious result of sitting in meditation. As for the efficacy of investigating Chan, you can experience it for yourself. You can return the light and illuminate within and ask yourself, "Am I still as gluttonous as I was before practicing Chan sitting? Am I still as materialistic as before? Have I corrected my improper habits and shortcomings? If I meet with unreasonable circumstances or matters that go against my wishes, do thoughts of affliction still arise?" If the answers are "yes", then I can tell you that you have not progressed much from sitting in Chan. If you can reduce past bad habits and shortcomings, then you have some good news in your cultivation skill.

You can examine yourself as follows:

(1) Let us take a look at eating, for instance. If you could eat both tasty and non-tasty food with the same state of mind, then you would have chased away the greedy ghost.

(2) Performing tasks: Is it the case that we will do anything that is beneficial to us and that we will not do anything that does not benefit ourselves? Are we very lazy, always seeking ease and comfort? If so, our skill in Chan samadhi has not improved. If you could change and be willing to do whatever might benefit others, and focus on being of service to the multitudes while not paying attention to your own personal matters, then you could get rid of the lazy ghost. If you could become more energetic day by day and were not always in a daze, then you could chase away the sleepy ghost.

If you can chase away the greedy ghost, lazy ghost and sleepy ghost, then you gain preliminary skill in Chan meditation. In this way, your spirit and temperament will definitely be quite different from the past and you will undergo a great change in personality. As the saying goes, "*In the same temple but a different god*". It can also be said "*In the same temple but a different ghost*". In the past, you were a ghost king, but now you are a Bodhisattva. Perhaps, you had an evil heart in the past but now you have the heart of a Bodhisattva.

Demonic power causes you to think of retreating.

All of you should realize that cultivating the spiritual path is not an easy matter. If you decide to cultivate, then demons will come around. They will not come from only one direction, they will come from all directions at once. There are demons of sickness, demons of vexation, demons in the heavens, human demons, and also demonic ghosts. There are demonesses as well. Demons appear from places that you do not expect to disturb you so that your resolve will waver and your cultivation will falter. They use many tricks to seduce and tempt you. They also threaten you, trying to get you to retreat in fear. They hope your samadhi power will vanish and your resolve for the spiritual path will disappear.

States may be false or true.

Just about the time your meditation is starting to have some success, the demons appear to test your resolve and to challenge your work in the spiritual path. They may appear as a very beautiful woman or a handsome man who comes to seduce you. If the sight does not disturb you, then you pass your test. But if you are distracted by this illusion, you will fall. Right there is the critical moment. Just that is the test. So I exhort you at all costs, do not fail such tests. If you fail, then once you fall, you will regret it forever. When states arise to challenge your resolve, you should test the state to see whether or not it is true. What should your method of testing be? It is very simple. Just recite the name of Amitabha Buddha. Recite with single-minded, unwavering concentration. If it is a false state, then it will gradually disappear until it vanishes completely. If it is a true state, then the longer you recite, the clearer the state will grow. Chan meditators who do not understand this method will fall into the demons' traps. They will fall among the demons and their work in the spiritual path will be scattered and lost. Such cultivators will lose their opportunity for enlightenment after they join the demons.

As soon as you cultivate the spiritual path, demons will appear.

When I was young, I heard someone said, "As soon as you cultivate the spiritual path, demons will appear." I did not believe it and arrogantly said, "I am not afraid of demons at all! Witches, ghosts, and goblins do not frighten me in the least." I thought that it did not matter what I said. Who could have guessed that soon after my boast, a demon would show up? What kind of demon was it? It was a demon of sickness, which made me so ill that I lost consciousness for seven or eight days. I lapsed into a total coma. Only then did I realize that my skill was far from the mark and that I had failed my test.

Maybe I was not afraid of witches, ghosts or goblins, or even celestial demons and heretics. But I was afraid, as it turned out, of sickness demons. I could not subdue them. I could not handle them. I could not endure their attack. So we cultivators of the spiritual path cannot claim proudly that we fear nothing. As soon as we become self-satisfied and arrogant, troubles come seeking for us.

Well, how should cultivators of the spiritual path be, then? We should maintain a humble and circumspect attitude, and be as cautious as if we were treading on the brink of a deep abyss, or as if we were standing on thin ice. At all times, we should be prudent and careful. We should pay attention and stay alert. Only then can we really cultivate the spiritual path. To sum it up, talk less and meditate more. This is the fundamental requisite of cultivation.

If we awaken to what we see, we can transcend the mundane world.

When cultivators of the spiritual path actually gain some accomplishment, they get it with someone's help. Who helps them? Demons bring cultivators to accomplishment. This is just like a knife being honed on a whetstone, so that it becomes very sharp. When a cultivator realizes the light of wisdom, it is with the help of the demons. Thus, we can look upon demons as Dharma-protectors who help us in reverse. There is a saying:

> *If we awaken to what we see,*
> *we can transcend the mundane world.*
> *If we are confused by what we see,*
> *then we will continue to transmigrate.*

With samadhi power,
we need not fear demons.

If we can awaken to and understand states as they appear, then we can transcend this mundane world. If we do not awaken and are instead confused by states as they occur, then we may fall so far that we end up in the hells. Cultivators of the spiritual path should not fear the presence of demons. We need only fear that our own concentration power will be insufficient to withstand them. We should realize that demons can help us along. They test us to see whether or not our spiritual skill is genuine and to see whether or not our samadhi power can endure them. If we have skill and samadhi, then no matter what demon comes, it will not be able to shake us.

By neither hurrying nor slacking off, we will succeed.

When practicing Chan meditation, we must not be too hurried. But we must also not slack off. If we are too hurried, we run the risk of overdoing it. If we slack off, we will fail to apply enough effort. Cultivating the spiritual path requires holding to the Middle Way. There is a saying,

> *Hurrying makes things too tight.*
> *Slacking off lets things get too loose.*
> *By not hurrying and not slacking off,*
> *We can succeed at what we do.*

If we apply effort in this way every day and in every moment, without hurrying or slacking off, eventually our skill will generate a response. When this happens, we will achieve an inconceivable state. Those of you who have attained this state should not be overly happy, and those who have not, should not be unduly sad. If a practitioner becomes overly happy, a demon of happiness can come and disrupt his samadhi power, causing that person to laugh and smile unnaturally all day long. If somebody asks him what he is laughing about, he will not know.

If he does not even know why he is laughing, then basically he has lost his senses. He has gone mad. A demon of madness has already possessed him. Conversely, if a practitioner becomes excessively sad, worried, or depressed, a demon of sadness can come and disrupt her samadhi power, causing her to sob and cry unnaturally all day long. If someone asks her why she is crying, she may reply, "Beings are suffering so much! They are so pitiful! I wish to cross over all beings." However, if she cannot even cross over herself, how can she possibly save others? Excessive displays of sorrow are an indication that a person has been possessed by a demon of sadness.

Do not be moved by sounds.

When we sit in meditation, we should not be moved by sounds or be turned by forms. Some people may have cultivated for a long time, but when states arise, they attach to them. We should not do that. We should hear without listening. We should see without perceiving. Not listening and not perceiving, we will not be moved by states.

Do not harbor thoughts of hatred and love.

As all dharmas are the Buddhadharma, how could there be some dharmas that we like and some that we dislike? In investigating Chan, we should work on this very thing. We should not harbor thoughts of hatred and love, but should instead bring our minds to a state of equanimity. In a still spring pond, undisturbed even by ripples, silt will naturally settle to the bottom and the water will become clear. Investigating Chan is also like that. If no ripples of false thoughts stir in our minds, then the Dharma-body will manifest.

The Dharma I have just spoken is very important. I hope that all of you will cultivate according to this principle, for if you do, you will very quickly open your wisdom.

> *What is spoken is the Dharma.*
> *Practice of it is the Way.*

105

If we understand the Dharma and yet do not cultivate the Way, we will not make any progress.

No matter what happens, remain in unmoving suchness.

When we sit in meditation, all kinds of different states may arise. Regardless of whether a state is wholesome or unwholesome, we should not pay too much attention to it. If we pay attention to it, we will be turned by the state. If we can just ignore it, then we will not be turned by it. Sometimes, Chan cultivators may feel as if they are as large as empty space. At other times, they may feel that they are even smaller than a speck of dust. There are occasions when they feel as though their bodies no longer exist, and they do not know where they have gone. Sometimes, they may feel unbearably cold. At other times, they may feel unbearably hot. Sometimes, they feel that their bodies are harder and stronger than vajra. At other times, their bodies may feel as soft and light as cotton. Sometimes, they may feel their bodies charged with energy akin to electricity. At other times, they may feel that they are emitting bright light. In a nutshell, such states are boundless and endless, but we should not become attached to any of them. If we become attached to them, then we may enter a demonic state. As long as we remain unattached, we will not have any problem. The *Shurangama Sutra* says that whatever states arise, if we do not discriminate and instead act as if nothing is happening, then we will be fine. However, if we decide that we must be special to be able to experience such a terrific state, we will fall and become possessed by a demon. Whatever states we encounter, we must remain unmoved. Eventually, we will enter unmoving suchness and gain samadhi power that is perfectly clear and constantly bright. Then, no matter what happens, we will be able to turn the state around instead of being turned by it.

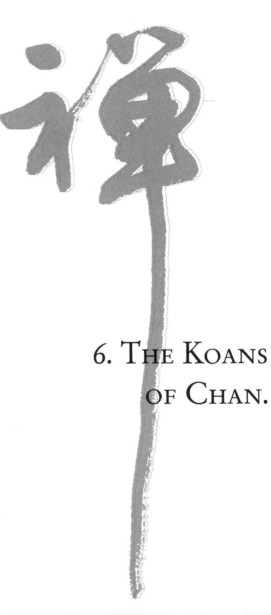

6. THE KOANS
OF CHAN.

A Golden Pagoda, a Silver Pagoda, a Muddy Heap

By sitting in the full lotus posture, we generate precept power, samadhi power, and wisdom power. The Vajra Dharma-protectors will protect those who sit in full lotus. The demon kings will be kept at bay, and the hungry ghosts will make obeisance.

Here is a koan about full lotus posture. In the past, when Buddhism prevailed in China, monks would be invited to recite sutras at funerals and other special events. Monks who crassly made a profession out of this were derisively referred to as sutra-peddlers. This story is about one such monk who made a living peddling sutras. Once, it was nearing midnight when he set out on his return from an evening of chanting sutras for a fee. As he passed through the village, a dog barked at him. The owners of the dog wondered why their dog was barking. The lady of the house said, "Take a look and see who it is. Is it a thief trying to steal something?" Her husband looked out of the window and said, "Oh, it is nothing. Just that sutra-peddling ghost. Just a sutra-peddling ghost." The monk became perplexed when he heard that comment. "Why did he refer to me as a sutra-peddling ghost?" He considered himself to be a sutra-reciting monk, but that man had called him the sutra-peddling ghost. He walked on, intent on getting back to his monastery. Suddenly, there was a cloudburst, and the rain poured down. Quickly, the monk took shelter under a bridge. With nothing else to do, he sat down to meditate. Just as he pulled his legs into full lotus posture, two ghosts emerged from the river. Those ghosts were terribly ugly. Normally, if someone sees a ghost, he will be alarmed. But since the monk was meditating, he was not afraid when he saw the two ghosts. Besides, since he often chanted sutras to cross over ghosts, he thought a lot about ghosts. Hence, when he met these two, he was not afraid. He just kept meditating.

Well, the two ghosts started bowing to him. They kept on bowing to him for somewhere between twenty minutes and half an hour. After that stretch of time, the monk's legs began to hurt, and he could not endure sitting in full lotus any longer. And so, he eased out of full lotus position into half lotus. Then he heard the two ghosts talking, "Hey, just now we were bowing to a golden pagoda. How did it become a silver one?"

Now it became clear to the monk why the ghosts were bowing to him. Since pagodas contain sharira [jewel-like relics that remain after cremation] of Buddhas and sages, when ghosts see a pagoda, they must bow and pay respect. "They must be seeing a pagoda here," thought the monk in amazement.

Well, after what the ghosts perceived as a golden pagoda became a silver one, one of the ghosts said, "There are also sharira in silver pagodas, so we had better keep bowing to pay our respects!" With that, the two ghosts started bowing again. Meanwhile, the monk sat for another half hour or so in the half-lotus position before his legs began to hurt again. Finally, he could endure the pain no longer. But the rain had not stopped. If it had, he would have left his shelter under the bridge and continued on his way. To ease the pain in his legs, the monk moved into a casual cross-legged sitting position. Well, when the two ghosts took a peek, they simultaneously exclaimed, "Look! This is not a golden pagoda or a silver one. It is just a heap of mud! Let us destroy it!"

As soon as the monk heard that the ghosts were going to attack him, he quickly pulled his legs back up and sat in a full lotus position again. The ghosts perceived the heap of mud turn into a golden pagoda again. "Wow! What an awesome state! We had better bow some more." So, they started bowing to the pagoda again.

Thereupon the monk thought to himself, "Hmmm... Full lotus position creates a golden pagoda. Half lotus creates a silver pagoda. Sitting casually is just a mound of mud." Here he was a human being, but those ghosts saw him as a mound of mud. How strange!

From that time on, the monk resolved to attain Bodhi and no longer went around peddling sutras. He stopped chanting sutras for a livelihood. Instead, he practiced meditation in his monastery, always in a full lotus position. After sitting for some time, he became enlightened, whereupon he reflected, "My enlightenment was actually helped along by those two ghosts. If I had not met them, I would not be enlightened today." So after that, he called himself Pressured by Ghosts. That is the name we know him by today: Chan Master Pressured by Ghosts. The ghosts forced him into cultivating.

Seeking a Method to Avoid Death

The Chan sect has a verse that says,

> *The myriad dharmas return to One.*
> *The One returns to the origin.*
> *Shen Guang, not understanding this,*
> *Pursued Master Bodhidharma.*
> *He knelt nine years at Bear's Ear Mountain,*
> *Hoping for a method to avoid King Yama.*

Seeking the Dharma is not an easy task. It requires a spirit of sacrifice. Here is a story about that.

After traveling by boat from India to China, Patriarch Bodhidharma came ashore at Guangzhou and went north to Nanjing. Passing by the place where Dharma Master Shen Guang was lecturing the sutras, the patriarch went in to join the assembly.

After the lecture, the patriarch asked Master Shen Guang, "What are you doing here?"

Master Shen Guang answered "I am lecturing on the sutras."

Patriarch Bodhidharma asked, "Why are you explaining the sutras?"

Master Shen Guang replied, "In order to teach people how to end birth and death."

Patriarch Bodhidharma replied, "The essence of Dharma cannot be put into words. There is no Dharma to be spoken of. As to the sutras you lecture, the inked areas are words and the blank areas are paper. How can this end birth and death?"

When Master Shen Guang heard that, he became angry and shouted, "You devil! How dare you slander the Buddha, Dharma, and Sangha. This is outrageous!" Then he struck Patriarch Bodhidharma on the face with his iron chanting beads!

The patriarch was caught unprepared and two of his front teeth got broken off. Patriarch Bodhidharma thought to himself, "If I spit the teeth on the ground, then this place will suffer three years of great drought." [The folk belief was that if the teeth of a certified sage fell to the ground, the heavens would mete out punishment and the region would suffer a three-year drought.] Patriarch Bodhidharma did not wish to let this region's people go through the suffering of a drought, so he swallowed the two teeth instead of spitting them out. His decision accords with the saying,

If someone knocks out the teeth of an arhat, the arhat swallows them.

Patriarch Bodhidharma practiced the paramita of patience under insult. Without a word, he left Master Shen Guang's lecture hall. He crossed the Yangtze River and headed toward the Song Mountain Range in Henan Province.

At that time, the Ghost of Impermanence, under the orders of King Yama, came to invite Master Shen Guang to a tea in the underworld.

He asked the monk, "Are you Shen Guang?"

Master Shen Guang replied, "Yes."

The Ghost of Impermanence said, "King Yama sent me to invite you down for tea."

Master Shen Guang was surprised and said, "When I lecture on the sutras, the heavens rain down flowers, and golden lotuses well forth from the earth. Yet I still have to die?"

The Ghost of Impermanence said, "Of course you have to die!"

Master Shen Guang questioned, "Who in this world is free from death?"

The Ghost of Impermanence told him, "That black-faced monk whose teeth you knocked out is free from death."

Master Shen Guang then implored the Ghost of Impermanence saying, "Mr. Impermanence, could you be compassionate and speak to King Yama, asking him to let me go and find the dark-faced monk so that I can learn the method for ending birth and death?"

The Ghost of Impermanence agreed to his request. Master Shen Guang then headed north, traveling day and night in order to catch up with Patriarch Bodhidharma. Finally, he arrived at Bear's Ear Mountain and saw Patriarch Bodhidharma sitting in a cave facing the wall in meditation.

He bowed to Patriarch Bodhidharma in repentance. After nine years of kneeling, Master Shen Guang obtained a method to avoid death, and became the Second Patriarch of the Chan School in China.

Enlightenment must be certified before it counts.

Before the time of the Buddha Awesome Voice, anyone who became enlightened did not need to be certified by another person. But after the time of the Buddha Awesome Voice, enlightenment has to be certified before it counts. Someone who thinks he or she has become enlightened must have that enlightenment certified by a Patriarch or bright-eyed Good and Wise Advisor. For example, *The Shurangama Sutra* contains the stories of twenty-five sages who each describe how they gained perfect enlightenment, and who then each request Shakyamuni Buddha to certify their attainments.

I will now tell a story of such a certification. During the Tang Dynasty of China, a Great Master called Yongjia (Eternal Excellence) was born in Yongjia county of Zhejiang Province. Because he stayed in Yongjia all his life, people gave him the name of

119

Great Master Yongjia. After he entered monastic life, he studied the teachings of the Tian Tai School and cultivated meditative contemplation. One day, while reading *The Vimalakirti Nirdesa Sutra*, he suddenly got enlightened. Soon after, he met a disciple of the Sixth Patriarch named Chan Master Xuance (Mystic Law) and related his awakening. Master Xuance suggested that he go to Cao Creek to pay respects to the Sixth Patriarch and request certification of his enlightenment. To do otherwise, to claim that one has become enlightened by oneself without the benefit of a teacher, would make one a follower of the externalists who believe in spontaneity.

When he arrived at Nanhua Monastery in Cao Creek, the Sixth Patriarch was meditating. Master Yongjia, full of pride, strode directly in front of the Patriarch's meditation seat. Without even making a half bow, let alone a full prostration, he simply grasped his tin staff, walked three times around the Patriarch's seat, then stood and rapped his staff on the ground.

The Sixth Patriarch said, "Shramanas (monks) ought to possess the Three Thousand Modes of Awesome Deportment, and the Eighty Thousand Subtle Manners. Only when one's behavior is impeccable does one merit the name Shramana. [Shramana means 'diligent and putting to rest'. A Shramana 'diligently cultivates precepts, concentration, and wisdom, and puts to rest greed, hatred, and stupidity.'] Where do you, O Virtuous One, come from? And why are you so arrogant?"

Master Yongjia answered, "Birth and death is the only important thing, and impermanence comes with haste."

The Sixth Patriarch said, "Then why do you not embody birthlessness. Why do you not understand 'no-haste'?"

Master Yongjia answered, "Once I understood, there is no birth. Once I realized it, there is no haste."

The Sixth Patriarch said, "You have really grasped the idea of birthlessness."

Master Yongjia said, "Do you mean to say that birthlessness is an idea?"

The Sixth Patriarch said, "If it is not an idea, then how can you distinguish it?"

Master Yongjia said, "Making distinctions is not an idea, either."

"You are so right! You are so right!" said the Sixth Patriarch, and thereupon certified him and made him his Dharma heir.

After Great Master Yongjia was certified by the Sixth Patriarch, he planned to return immediately to Kaiyuan (Primary Source) Monastery in Yongjia. The Sixth Patriarch asked him to stay for one night, but the next morning, he went right back to Yongjia. Because his enlightenment to the truth of the Buddhadharma was certified in just a single evening, people of that time nicknamed him, "The Monk Who Became Enlightened Overnight". Afterwards, he energetically propagated the Sudden Teaching of the Chan School and is most noted for his *Song of Enlightenment* of more than fifty stanzas, which explains the state of sudden enlightenment. The Song is a masterpiece that will long endure and has become required reading for Buddhists.

How Chan Meditation Can Halt the Process of Birth and Death

In the final years of the Northern Song Dynasty in China, there lived a national hero, Yue Fei. His father passed away when he was young. His mother was worthy and wise. Mother and son had only each other to rely upon for support. She taught her young son to read and write. Since the family was too poor to afford brushes, ink and paper, he practiced writing characters in the sand, and eventually became an accomplished calligrapher. Yue Fei entered military service at an early age. His mother tattooed on his back the slogan, "Give your all in service to the country". He never forgot his great vow to save his country's people.

This was the era when the Tartars (of the Jin Dynasty) invaded the Song Dynasty and captured the capital of Bianjing (Kaifeng). They kidnapped the two Emperors Hui and Qin and took them to the North.

123

Duke Kang established the Southern Song Dynasty in Hangzhou and proclaimed himself Emperor Gaozong. He appointed Qin Hui as his Prime Minister. At that time, the scholars advocated peace, while the military advocated going to war with the Tartars. General Yue Fei gave the Tartars a devastating defeat at the town of Zhuxian (close to Bianjing) and planned to attack their capital towards Yellow Dragon (near Jilin Nongan). Unfortunately, Prime Minister Qin Hui was jealous of Yue Fei and so issued twelve false summons commanding Yue Fei to return to the capital. Yue Fei's credo was 'loyal subjects are patriots to the end'. Thus he led his troops back to the capital. En route he passed by Gold Mountain Monastery, in the middle of the Yangtze River, where he stopped to pay his respects to Chan Master Daoyue (Joy of the Way).

The monk urged him not to return to the capital, but to enter monastic life and cultivate the Way at Gold Mountain Monastery in Zhenjiang. That way, he could avoid all political scandals and conflict. Yue Fei did not take the matter of birth and death seriously, feeling instead that the duty of a military man was to follow orders. He did not follow the philosophy that, "When the general is in the field, he can choose not to follow the emperor's commands". Thus, he rejected Master Daoyue's wise suggestion.

Before he left, Master Daoyue wrote him a verse that said,

Before the New Year's Day,
    be very cautious of heaven's tears.
A gift with two dots beneath it
    will harm you grievously.

Yue Fei returned to Hangzhou and Qin Hui sent a
message to his military reading "No grounds necessary",
which was a summon to imprison both Yue Fei and
his son. As he approached the executioner's block, Yue
Fei suddenly realized the meaning hidden in Venerable
Daoyue's verse. On New Year's Eve, which fell on the
twenty-ninth day of the twelfth lunar month that year,
the heavens poured forth a heavy rain. Hearing the rain
as he sat in jail, Yue Fei knew his death was at hand. The
prophecy in the Chan Master's verse was about to be
fulfilled. When you write two dots beneath the word
'gift', you get the word 'Qin', the name of Prime Minister
Qin Hui. Yue Fei was executed at Fengbo Pagoda.

Qin Hui asked the executioner what Yue Fei's final
words had been. The executioner said, "I heard him say,
'I have met my end today, only because I did not heed
the advice of Chan Master Daoyue of Gold Mountain.'"
Qin Hui flew into a rage and ordered Heli to hurry to
Gold Mountain Monastery to arrest Master Daoyue.
But the day before, while in Chan samadhi, Master
Daoyue had foreseen this situation and had written
another verse, which said,

Heli is coming from the South,
But I am going to the West.
If my strength in the Dharma
  were not sufficient,
I would surely have fallen
  into the villain's hands.

After he wrote this verse, he entered the stillness of Nirvana. When Heli reached the temple the next day, Master Daoyue had already entered Nirvana. Heli had no choice but to return to the capital and make a report.

This story proves that when you have perfected the skill of Chan meditation, you can control your own birth and death. You can go off to rebirth at any time you choose. You are in control of the process, and it is a very natural matter.

Chan Masters of the past all possessed this ability. They could be born and die as they wished. In the Tang Dynasty, there was a Chan Master named Deng Yinfeng (Hidden Summit) who entered Nirvana while standing on his head. The contemporary monk, the Living Buddha of Gold Mountain, entered Nirvana while standing up. Due to their skill in Chan meditation, they could come and go as they pleased, without any restrictions.

The mind of Elder Master Wei Shan did not move.

Venerable Master Lingyou Wei Shan of the Tang Dynasty cultivated the Way on Wei Mountain of Hunan Province. There, he gained the samadhi power that enabled him to instantly reach stillness when he sat. He was detached completely from all manner of wealth, relatives, friends, and the five sensual desires. Although Venerable Master Wei Shan did not seek fame and fortune, everyone came to know about his cultivation as time went by. As a result, many people came to give offerings and to draw near him, with the hope of seeking blessings and wisdom. His good reputation even spread to the ears of Prime Minister Pei Xiu, who then went to call upon him. On the mountain, the Prime Minister saw that there was only a simple hut without even a bed. There was only a sitting cushion and the old venerable simply sat there. When people came, he did not move and when people left, he did not acknowledge either. He ignored all visitors, neither receiving them nor seeing them off.

Prime Minister Pei Xiu thought, "This old cultivator does not even have a monastery. Since I am wealthy, I might as well make an offering to him so he can build a monastery!" He then ordered his followers to take out three hundred taels of silver. However, Venerable Master Wei Shan neither accepted the offering nor rejected it. There was a clump of grass near the hut and so Prime Minister Pei Xiu hid the silver in it. At that time, three hundred taels of silver was equivalent to about three million dollars now.

Three years later, Prime Minister Pei Xiu thought, "The monastery should be completed by now. Let us go and take a look!" When he arrived at the mountain, he found that there was nothing but the same old hut. No monastery had been built. Prime Minister Pei Xiu then had a false thought, "I gave him money, yet he did not use it to build a monastery and he still appears impoverished. Who knows where the money has gone?" Thereupon, he asked Venerable Master Wei Shan, "Chan Master! Where is the money that I gave you to build a monastery?" Venerable Master Wei Shan replied, "Look for it where you left it." Pei Xiu walked to the clump of grass and found that the money was still there untouched. Then Pei Xiu had another false thought, "This old cultivator is really lazy. I gave him money and yet he does not even know how to use it. Why is it that the more he cultivates, the more stupid he becomes?" At this point, Venerable Master Wei Shan told him, "Since you think that I do not know how to use money, you had better take it back and spend it on other things. I am not interested in building a monastery that has physical form."

Pei Xiu then realized that this Chan master had some substance, and so resolved to build the monastery for him. He built the physical monastery, but did not know the importance of nurturing the incomparable wisdom of his own mind. Venerable Master Wei Shan did know, and was building an inner monastery of wisdom. If we can silence our mind, quiet our thoughts, and not seek the five desires, then we can also be true cultivators. We should all learn from Venerable Master Wei Shan and not be moved by the sight of money.

An old monk in meditation
is worth ten thousand
taels of gold.

Elder Master Wei Shan once said, "An old monk in meditation is worth ten thousand taels of gold." Prime Minister Pei Xiu knew that entering monastic life was good, but due to his position as premier, he could not leave the home-life. Instead, he built a great monastery that could accommodate two thousand monks cultivating together. At that time, many monastics heard of the new Way-place at Hunan and flocked there to draw near and learn from Elder Master Lingyou of Wei Shan, who taught Chan meditation and gave talks on the precepts and the Vinaya every day.

Prime Minster Pei Xiu, knowing that he was not destined for monkhood, sent his son to the monastery to become a monk. This son was a Hanlin scholar, a graduate of the country's highest institution of learning. Venerable Master Wei Shan, observing that this Hanlin scholar had come to enter monastic life, named him Fa Hai and assigned him to fetch water. At that time, there were often a few thousand occupants at the monastery and this job was not easy. There was no tap water and water had to be drawn from the wells from morning until night without stop.

Fa Hai woke up at three o'clock in the morning, and while the Great Assembly was doing the morning recitation, he had already started fetching water. He fetched water like this for several years and did not do any other tasks. He did not even attend any sutra chanting or meditation session. Being a Hanlin scholar, fetching water for the Great Assembly might have seemed unfair to him, but he never complained and just did his best.

One day, it so happened that he had some free time. As he had never known what sort of lessons the monks actually studied, he sneaked into the Chan Hall and took a peek. He saw some monks sitting in an upright posture, and some sitting with their heads lowered, snoring in their sleep.

Others had their eyes open and were looking around. Fa Hai thought, "I carry water every day, working myself to exhaustion and here they are, some sleeping while sitting and others looking around with their eyes wide open. How can these monks be worthy of my offering?!" So he complained in his heart.

Fa Hai harbored these thoughts and although he did not tell anyone, Master Wei Shan knew what was up. He called Fa Hai to the Abbot's quarters and said, "You have stayed in this monastery for a few years only but now you complain that the monks are not fit to receive offerings from you. As of now, this monastery will not keep you anymore. You can pack your things and go!"

His teacher had kicked him out! When Fa Hai went to bid farewell to his teacher, he asked, "Master, I have no money. Where can I go?"

Chan Master Lingyou then gave him coins amounting to eight-and-a-half cents and told him, "You can go wherever you wish. When you have finished using the eight-and-a-half cents, then stay at that place. Do not stop until you have used up the money." At the time, eight-and-a-half cents was equivalent to eighty-five dollars now, which was not much. While on the road, Fa Hai did not dare use any of the money. He begged for alms along the way and traveled from Hunan to Jiangsu Province. Later, he passed by Zhenjiang and saw an island in the Yangtze River. There was a mountain on the island. Fa Hai wished to take a look at the mountain and so waved at the ferryman and asked for the price of the ferry trip.

The ferryman asked for exactly eight-and-a-half cents-no more, no less! When Fa Hai arrived at the mountain, he found that although it was not very high, it was serene and quiet. So he decided to settle down there. Later, he discovered a cave in the mountain. In the cave, he found jars filled with gold. That is how the mountain became known as Gold Mountain. Fa Hai used the gold to build a monastery and continued his Chan practice there.

Since then, Gold Mountain's atmosphere of cultivation has been exceptionally good and has produced many patriarchs. At that time, he had not yet received the full precepts and was still a novice monk, but he was already a founding patriarch.

Venerable Master Wei Shan's famous words, *'An old monk in meditation is worth ten thousand taels of gold'*, is referring to Fa Hai. Fa Hai felt that the monks were not fit to accept his offerings, but that was not true. When a person sits in meditation, he will eventually experience ultimate stillness, and light will penetrate everywhere. It is also said,

> *Sitting perfectly still in meditation*
> *for even a split second,*
> *Generates merit that surpasses that of*
> *building pagodas of the seven gems*
> *in number like the Ganges' sands.*

That is the reason a meditator is worth ten thousand taels of gold. A student of Buddhism who hopes to attain Buddhahood must practice Chan meditation. Practice diligently and do not be afraid when your legs hurt and

your back aches. In that way you will have some success.
An old saying goes:

> *If the plum tree did not endure*
> *cold that chills to the bone,*
> *How could the fragrance*
> *of its blossoms be so sweet?*

Do not be attached to states.

While meditating, the combination of the four elements of earth, water, fire, and wind, of which we are all composed, can all enter samadhi. They can enter the samadhi of emptiness or the samadhi of neither thought nor non-thought. While we are in samadhi, we should not become attached to states and should not allow ignorance and afflictions to move us. If we do, our chances of becoming enlightened will be obstructed. Let me tell you another koan to illustrate this.

In the past, there was an old cultivator who wanted to be born in the Heaven of Neither Thought nor Non-thought, the highest heaven in the formless realm. And so he cultivated the samadhi of neither thought nor non-thought. He was cultivating on a seashore, and was just about to enter the samadhi of neither thought nor non-thought, when the noise of a

135

fish playing in the water disturbed him so that he could not enter samadhi. When he opened his eyes, the fish immediately swam away. He then continued meditating, and just when he was about to enter samadhi, the fish swam back again. This happened many times and caused the old cultivator to feel terribly frustrated. Anger welled and he thought, "I wish I could turn into a kingfisher and eat up all the fish in the water!" His hatred scared the fish away and it dared not come again.

The old cultivator finally managed to enter the samadhi of neither thought nor non-thought, and was reborn in the Heaven of Neither Thought nor Non-thought, where he enjoyed eighty thousand great eons of heavenly bliss.

But because of that fit of anger he had in which he said he wished he could become a bird that ate fish, when his heavenly blessings came to an end, he immediately became a kingfisher. It was only when Shakyamuni Buddha had attained Buddhahood, and later expounded the Dharma to him, that he was able to discard the body of a kingfisher and be reborn as a human being. He then cultivated under the Buddha and attained Arhatship.

This koan shows why cultivators should not casually get angry, as false thoughts will surely receive retribution.

In the *Shurangama Sutra*, a Bodhisattva named

Moonlight specialized in cultivating water samadhi. He contemplated water, and when he entered the samadhi of water-radiance, his body would turn into water.

Once, when Moonlight Bodhisattva was in the water-radiance samadhi, his young disciple came to look for him. Upon entering his room, the disciple saw only a puddle of water on the floor. The mischievous disciple then picked up a small stone and threw it into the water. When Moonlight Bodhisattva came out of samadhi, he felt pain in his stomach and, upon investigation, discovered that there was a small stone inside it. He called his disciple and, questioning him, found out that the child had come into his room while he was in samadhi and had thrown a stone into the puddle he saw there. The teacher then instructed his disciple to wait until he entered samadhi again and then come into the room to retrieve the stone.

This koan shows us that as long as a cultivator practices with focused concentration and vigor, he will surely succeed. Cultivation requires one to be focused in order to be effective. If our mind remains firm and determined, we will definitely receive a response from the Dharma.

Chan Meditation -
It is Hard! It is Easy!

"Hard! Hard! Hard!
It is like trying to put ten baskets of sesame seeds
on the leaves of a tree in the yard."

That is how Elder Pang described cultivation. He thought it was not easy. If it did not lead to a backache, then it created pain in the legs. Cultivators experience all sorts of pain and suffering that make it hard to be at ease. It is with great difficulty that one manages to make a little progress. What is more, if we ever let down our guard, all our past efforts will be wasted. That was why Mr. Pang described practice as being like trying to balance lots of sesame seeds on the leaves of a tree. Ten baskets is not a small number, and to place the seeds on the leaves so that they stay there and do not fall off is not an easy thing to do. Mr. Pang had a relative who heard this and asked, "If it is that difficult, then is it not impossible to succeed in cultivation?"

Mrs. Pang responded,

> *"Easy! Easy! Easy!*
> *The Mind from the West, the patriarchs' intent,*
>   *appears right here on the tip of each blade of grass.*
> *Don't you see?"*

She said cultivation is actually very easy. All the mountains, rivers, flowers, grass and trees express the intention of the Patriarch's coming from the west. So she found it very easy. Not at all difficult.

Someone then asked Miss Pang, the daughter, what she thought about cultivation. She said,

> *"It is not easy. Nor is it hard.*
> *Just eat when hungry and sleep when you are tired."*

The three of them had very different views about the underlying principle of practice.

Mr. Pang, Mrs. Pang, and Miss Pang were part of the same family, and yet they had different opinions. Here, people have come from all directions to attend this meditation retreat and similarly, everyone has got his or her own views. The best way to handle that situation is to talk less and apply more effort in your cultivation.

Neither Coming nor Going

When I was in Manchuria, China, I had a fellow cultivator who was originally a bandit. Once, when he was robbing someone's valuables, he was beaten and suffered an injury to his shoulder. Six months passed but still the wounded shoulder did not heal. At that time, he became repentant and realized his past wrongdoings. He decided to change his evil character and embrace goodness, and so he made a vow, "If my injury heals within a week, I will go to my parents' graves and observe filial piety." After a week, his injury was completed healed. He then fulfilled his vow by spending three years observing filial piety beside his parents' graves. As he was able to turn over a new leaf, his master gave him the name, Filial Son Yo.

Before Filial Son Yo left for his parents' graves, he bowed to Dharma Master Zongyi as his master. This

Dharma Master had extremely virtuous conduct and gained the respect of many. He even possessed spiritual penetrations. When Filial Son Yo started learning meditation and applying effort, demonic obstacles transformed into a fire dragon that clasped tightly around his waist and burnt him until he was red and painful. In the midst of the demon's attack, his master subdued the fire dragon. This dragon then took refuge under him and became Filial Son Yo's Dharma-protector.

During the first two and a half years that Filial Son Yo sat by his parents' graves, endless rainstorms flooded the fields and destroyed many crops.

Because of that, Filial Son Yo made a vow, "If the sky clears in three days, I shall cut off a piece of my own flesh as an offering to the heavens." Sure enough, the heavens accorded with his wish, and the skies cleared in less than three days. As he had promised, Filial Son Yo then cut off a piece of his own flesh as offering to the heavens. When the nearby residents and county officials heard about Filial Son Yo's offering, they came in droves and praised him without end.

About that time, a little bird flew near and sang, "Do more good deeds! Do more good deeds! Doing good deeds is so good!" That little bird stayed close to where Filial Son Yo was sitting for about three weeks before flying away. It was truly an inconceivable occurrence!

When Filial Son Yo had completed observing three years of filial piety at his parents' graves, he began giving talks at the local branch of the Path of Virtue Society and taught beings how to practice the Bodhisattva Path. Filial Son Yo was twenty-one years old when he vowed to uphold his filial duties. At that time, I was in my teens and was also observing filial piety at my mother's grave. This was why we admired each other.

One day, we happened to meet. We observed each other in silence for a long time. Finally, Filial Son Yo asked, "Who are you?"

I answered, "You should know who you are, but I do not know who I am."

Filial Son Yo asked again, "Where do you come from?"

I replied, "I come from where I came from."

I then asked him, "Where are you going?"

He only answered, "I have nowhere to go." He had nothing else to reply.

There is no place to come from and no place to go to, and so there is neither coming nor going. There is neither coming nor going, and yet there is coming and going. Coming is coming from the place that we came from, and going is going to the place where we are headed. One of the Buddha's ten names is 'Tathagata'

(Thus Come One). The *Vajra Sutra* says, 'The Tathagata does not come from anywhere, nor does he go anywhere. Therefore, he is called the Tathagata."

The Three Cart Patriarch

The main purpose of meditation is to eradicate all our past evil karma, regain our original wisdom, and bring our good roots to fruition. We must be patient, and that means not being afraid of hardship. When the sages of old sat in meditation, they could sit for thousands of years. I shall now relate a koan as an example.

During the Tang Dynasty, when Dharma Master Xuan Zhuang was on his way to India to obtain sutras, he encountered an old cultivator in meditation. Birds had built nests on his head and his clothes were torn and tattered. Dharma Master Xuan Zhuang rang his bell to bring the old fellow out of samadhi. The old cultivator asked, "Where do you come from?"

Dharma Master Xuan Zhuang replied, "I come from the Land of Tang and I am going to India to seek for sutras. What are you doing here?"

The old cultivator said, "I am waiting for Shakyamuni Buddha to come into the world. Then I am going to help him propagate the Buddhadharma."

Dharma Master Xuan Zhuang said, "Why are you still waiting for the Buddha to come into the world? Shakyamuni Buddha has already passed into Nirvana for more than a thousand years."

The old cultivator said, "Is that a fact! Well, in that case, I will wait for the next Buddha, Maitreya, to come into the world." Thereupon, he prepared to go back into samadhi.

Dharma Master Xuan Zhuang interrupted him and said, "I have a matter to discuss with you."

The old cultivator replied, "Do not disturb my peace. I do not want to interfere in worldly affairs."

Dharma Master Xuan Zhuang said, "This is not a personal matter. Although Shakyamuni Buddha has already entered Nirvana, his Dharma is still in the world. I want you to help me spread the Buddhadharma and continue the Buddha's wisdom life. Now, you go the Land of Tang and wait for me to return with the sutras, and then we shall propagate the Buddhadharma together. From here, go east and get reborn in the house with the yellow-tiled roof."

Before Dharma Master Xuan Zhuang set out for India to bring back the sutras, he made a prediction to Emperor Tai Zong saying, "The branches of the pine tree are now pointing to the west. When they point east, that means I have returned with the sutras." One day, Emperor Tai Zong noticed that all the tree branches were pointing to the east and he knew that Dharma Master Xuan Zhuang would return soon.

When Dharma Master Xuan Zang returned to Chang An, Emperor Tai Zong led all the court officials to the western gate to welcome him.

It was a grand reception, and the streets were thronging with people. When Dharma Master Xuan Zhuang met the Emperor, he immediately said,

"Congratulations, Your Majesty, on the birth of a prince."

But the emperor replied, "No. I didn't have a son while you were away."

The Dharma Master looked into the matter and found that the old cultivator had missed his mark and been reborn in a house with blue tiles, instead of yellow. The blue-tiled house belonged to the Defense Minister Yu Chi Kong. He was now the nephew of Yu Chi Kong. Dharma Master Xuan Zang urged Yu Chi Kong's nephew to leave home but was rejected. He then pleaded with the Emperor to issue an edict ordering the war minister's nephew to enter monastic life, explaining, "It is essential that he leaves home. So no matter what conditions he asks for, agree to all of them."

Immediately, the Emperor issued an edict ordering the war minister's nephew to leave home.

When the nephew of Yu Chi Kong received the imperial command to leave home, he set up three conditions, saying, "My first condition is this. Originally, Buddhism does not permit drinking wine. However, I do not wish to give up drinking wine. I expect that wherever I go, there will be a cart of wine following me." The Emperor knew that one of the five precepts in Buddhism prohibits consuming alcohol, but then, Master Xuan Zhuang had told him to agree to any conditions that the nephew might have. So the Emperor agreed to the first condition.

Encouraged, the nephew continued, "Now for my second condition. I was born in the home of a general and I am used to eating meat. After I become a monk, I must still have fresh meat to eat every day."

The Emperor knew for a fact that monastics do not eat meat, but since Master Xuan Zhuang had already told the Emperor to agree with any terms, Tai Zong therefore had to agree to this one as well.

The nephew pressed on, "Here is my third condition. All my life, I have been fond of beautiful women. So wherever I go, I must have a cart full of beauties accompanying me." The Emperor agreed to all three conditions.

When Yu Chi Kong's nephew left home, the entire

imperial court gave him a send-off to Da Xing Shan (Great Flourishing Goodness) Monastery to enter monastic life. On that day, the monastery's big bell was rung and the gigantic drum was beaten to welcome him. As soon as he heard the bell and drum, he had a sudden enlightenment and remembered that he was the old cultivator who had promised to help Dharma Master Xuan Zhuang propagate the Buddhadharma. The moment he obtained the knowledge of past lives, he gave up the three carts of wine, meat, and women.

He became Patriarch Kui Ji, the Second Patriarch of the Fa Xiang (Dharma Marks) School. But all his life he was also known as the Three Cart Patriarch.

He could read ten lines at a glance and could discern clearly what one hundred people talking at the same time were saying. Patriarch Kui Ji helped Dharma Master Xuan Zhuang translate the discourses of the Dharma Marks School. His skills were unsurpassed. He earned the name 'Master of One Hundred Discourses'.

When the old cultivator sat in meditation, he could sit for a few thousand years. Here, we sit for only twenty-one hours each day, which is really insignificant by comparison. We must learn to look upon all matters as being trifles and should not be attached to anything. Endure suffering and pain. It is only by enduring a moment of pain that we can achieve everlasting happiness. All of you should be courageous and vigorous and cultivate diligently. In this way, you will be able to overcome all obstacles.

Cast aside birth and death.

A long time ago, there was a diligent old cultivator who had attained some success. But then, a state came along to test his samadhi power. What kind of state was it? Whenever he meditated and was about to enter samadhi, a big stone would appear, dangling from a rope above his head. If the rope were to break, he would be smashed into a meat patty. He knew that this was only a state, and he ignored it. This happened every day. The stone would be there, dangling above his head. Because of that, he became very cautious in his meditation and dared not fall asleep. But he also could not enter samadhi.

After a few days, the state changed. Now, there was a rat on the rope from which the stone was dangling. The rat was gnawing on the rope. The rope had been thin to begin with and now that the rat was gnawing at it, the danger of the stone crashing down on the meditator increased dramatically. As a result of this state, the old cultivator dared not meditate there again.

Actually, such states are all illusions. No matter what states appear, cultivators should ignore them. We must cast aside life and death. If we live, we live. If we die, we die. Our resolve should be that we would rather die as a result of cultivating than to live without doing so. If we do not fear death and can put everything down, we will surely gain enlightenment. This old cultivator was afraid of death, and so he did not dare to continue his meditation. Once he stopped meditating, his skill did not improve, and he did not accomplish anything.

> *Off by a hair's breadth to start with,*
> *We will miss by a thousand miles in the end.*

When we cultivate, no matter what states we encounter, we must have the samadhi power to ignore them. By doing that, we will eventually experience some positive results and will be able to overcome obstacles. Once we have overcome the obstacles, we will receive some good news.

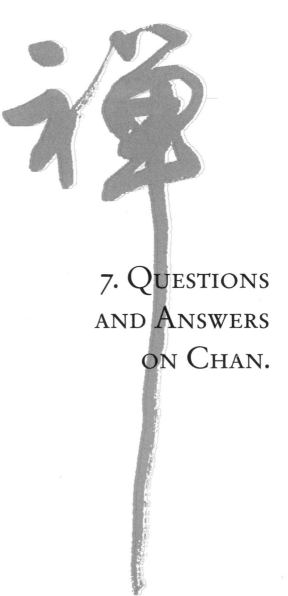

7. QUESTIONS AND ANSWERS ON CHAN.

Question: When we sit in meditation, what should our mind contemplate?

Venerable Master: There is no fixed place where the mind should be. You must find how to let your mind not dwell anywhere. If there is a location, your mind will reside there. Find out how to let the mind not reside anywhere and not think of good or bad. That is where you should apply effort. If you concentrate on a place and think of good and bad, then you are still caught up in attachments. In cultivating, we want to remain detached from everything. When there are no more attachments, we will even forget about our own body. If we are not even aware of our own body, what is left to attach to?

Question: Why must we sit in the full lotus position in order to enter samadhi? Are other methods acceptable? Is it all right to just sit still if we cannot bend our legs into that position?

Venerable Master: It is okay too. This position is the *vajra* position though, so it is stronger.

Question: Could the Venerable Master please point out the way for me? When someone is meditating, who or what is the meditator?

Venerable Master: You find out.

Question: What is the difference between entering samadhi and sleeping?

Venerable Master: Put simply, the posture of entering samadhi is to sit upright with your back straight and not tilt sideways. If your skill reaches the point where your breath stops or your pulse stops, you may appear to be as if dead, but you still have feelings. You can sit for a whole day without moving or for ten days without moving, or even sit for a month without moving. On the other hand, sleeping is different, because your head and body may recline and twist. You have no control over them in sleep. And when asleep, your breathing becomes heavier, so that your exhales and inhales often result in snoring. That is the basic difference between the two.

Question: Please tell us about the lotus posture.

Venerable Master: The sitting posture itself resembles a lotus. Also, sitting on a lotus all the time symbolizes that one's body is light and concentrated. It also represents the lotus in which the treasury of the worlds is located. These are reasons why this sitting position is known as the lotus posture. It is also called the auspicious position.

Question: Is the half-lotus sitting position analogous to a silver pagoda and the full lotus position to a gold pagoda?

Venerable Master: And, no position, no pagoda.

Question: What is the next step in meditation?

Venerable Master: The first requirements in meditation are to clear our minds and lessen our desires. A clear mind has no false thinking. Less desire means being less emotional.

Question: What is the primary purpose of meditation?

Venerable Master: The advantages to meditation are manifold. Whether we study, work, or take care of the house, daily meditation increases our concentration, lessens the pressures of life, and increases our physical health. If we honestly want to develop our wisdom and become liberated, then we must develop this habit. We must be committed to meditation for the long term, so that we can eventually be liberated from the cycle of birth and death.

Question: Is meditation a practice that tends to be more dangerous because one is more prone to being possessed by demons?

Venerable Master: There are different causes and conditions for this situation, not one. Some people cultivate and become possessed by demons more easily because they are extremely selfish, opinionated, and self-centered. These are the reasons why they cultivate.

Question: Meditators see illusions, as most people would call them. Could you please explain this phenomenon that occurs during meditation?

Venerable Master: Any phenomenon is illusory and false. What you see are just the fifty kinds of transformations according to the *Shurangama Sutra*. It would be very sad for you to consider any of these a form of accomplishment.

Question: What are the basics to Chan meditation?

Venerable Master: The basics are: 1. not being greedy; 2. not being angry; and 3. not being deluded.

Question: Our transcendental meditation instructor taught us to imagine a particular sound.

Venerable Master: That is a useless exercise, just like putting another head on top of a head or searching for a mule while riding on one.

Question: What happens when we feel pain during meditation?

Venerable Master: If you are aware of the pain, then take the attitude "the more pain, the better." If you cannot get past this stage, you will always hurt. Do not react to the signals of pain. You have to make it listen to you. You have to be the one in control. It helps to maintain the awareness that our body is not real, that it is a temporary combination of the four elements. In that sense, it is not of any great importance. We can reflect that if we were to die and go to the hells, we would experience agony in the hells that would be much more painful than this! We should ask ourselves what we can do now, while we are in control. We can decide to just let our body suffer a bit more, knowing that the pain is due to pressure being applied to our energy channels and circulatory system during meditation. We can remind ourselves that once we break through the obstructions, we will no longer experience pain.

Question: What is the difference between prayer and Chan meditation?

Venerable Master: If you think they are the same, then they are the same. If you think they are different, then they are different.

Question: I often hear people say that our soul can leave our body during meditation. What exactly is real meditation?

Venerable Master: Here is what the Honorable Ji said about meditation,

> *The gluttonous get hungry.*
> *The starved become lanky.*

Meditation is about stilling our thoughts. You will know when you are having an out-of-body experience during meditation. You also will know when you cannot leave your body. But do not dwell on either of those

159

experiences. I do not think about leaving my body or not leaving my body. I also am careful not to eat too much.

Question: You say that while we are meditating, we should be patient with what we feel. But I find that strange. Can we express our feelings, or should we keep them inside? Sometimes when I stuff them inside, I find that I want to explode afterwards. What should I do?

Venerable Master: Be patient with them, which means emptying them so that they disappear. It is not about hiding them inside. What is the use of hiding them inside? Why do you need to keep your garbage?

Forget them! Things that are suppressed can taint us more than anything. As powerful as the atom bomb may be, the power of suppression is even greater. If you are not afraid of exploding into pieces, go ahead and hide them. But I do not recommend it.

Question: Will you please help me with my meditation so that I can understand the principles of Buddhism even better, as well as those of other religions that I am studying?

Venerable Master: By sitting in meditation, we learn to take a beating. Sitting in meditation can be as painful as being beaten. This applies to the hours when we are not actually sitting as well. We ought to be patient when people hit us or yell at us. In general, we can meditate well and sleep in a sitting position when we are unaffected by the eight kinds of emotions.

Question: I am so stupid! 1) I cannot penetrate my own mind. 2) If I am not careful, I fall asleep when I meditate. How do I overcome these two problems?

Venerable Master: It is not so easy to penetrate the mind, especially in only two or three days. It is better to be asleep than to be having false thoughts.

Question: Is meditation and the "investigation of Dhyana" the same thing, or are they two different things?

Venerable Master: Although the terms are

different, they mean the same. If we really understand the investigation of Dhyana, then we will not be confused any longer.

Question: Venerable Master, please tell us the difference between our rules and the rules in the meditation centers of China.

Venerable Master: Obviously there are lots of differences. But here we must assert our independence and uniqueness. We only choose what is good and we discard what is wrong. We intend to reform the parts of Buddhism that only cause problems and bring no benefit.

Food: Meditators in China require three meals a day: porridge for breakfast, a full lunch, and stuffed buns for an evening snack.

Beatings: Every meditator has to be beaten in China. The proctor beats the participants one by one. You are beaten whether you act correctly or otherwise. The harder you are hit, the more the monastery gets to show how strict its rules are. Gaoming Monastery, for example, is famous for its beatings. Sometimes they break their incense board while beating people. None of you have been beaten yet this year. You have been hit in the past. I am probably more compassionate this year, and your karmic obstacles are lighter too. These are some of the differences. Those monks in China are really scary. They allow no trace of a smile on their face at all, looking as stern as Sangarama Bodhisattva. Were you to go into their Chan Halls, you would be too scared to even lift your head. It would be like a mouse seeing a cat.

We do not beat people for no reason here. I am pleasant and I give you talks every day as if I were babysitting. Yet you still have to suffer while you adjust to the sitting posture of meditation. Why do I think that letting you suffer is all right? People in this country have a tremendous amount of blessings. If I do not make you suffer a bit, you will not develop any major commitment to cultivating. You give up wearing nice clothes, eating good food, living in a nice house, and you forego all kinds of luxuries to come and suffer here.

This is the very best way to get rid of arrogance, so that we can honestly cultivate and become liberated from birth and death.

Rules: Also, you absolutely cannot stretch out your legs in the meditation halls of China. You will definitely get hit that way. They will not be a bit polite. The head of the hall gets beaten too if he violates the rules. For instance, if the head of the hall snoozes on occasion, the proctor will have to kneel on his right knee before hitting him, which is different than the posture he assumes in hitting the rest of the group.

Also, there is a certain way to hold one's teacup, because the cup has no handle. You have to place your thumb on the rim of the cup and use the rest of hand to hold the cup from the bottom. With your cup in hand, you extend your arm to let the attendant pour you tea. After you are done with the tea, you place the cup in front of you and the attendant will take it away. This is done in complete silence. We drink ginseng tea here, so our rules are substandard. We can study these rules and improve upon them over time. But we do not have to imitate China for sure. The rules have to fit the culture here. Meditators in China absolutely cannot go outside the hall to drink tea, to sit down, to stand around, and to chat. They return to the Chan hall for walking meditation immediately after their meal. They do not waste one second of their time. They do not do anything else at all in between. They do not go to rinse their mouths and or do some stretching after eating. We will change these little problems gradually, so that we stay on the right track.

Question: Is a demon that appears during one's meditation a creation of the mind? If it is made from the mind alone, is that the same kind of demon that you talked about earlier?

Venerable Master: When you have offended demons outside of you, the demons in you will also act up. There is not just one kind of demon and not just one kind of ghost. There are heavenly demons, earth demons, spiritual demons, ghostly demons, demons who are people, demons made from the mind, and demons that are created by external states. There is not just one kind, but many kinds.

Question: I studied transcendental meditation. While meditating, I would listen to a sound and visualize a scene by the ocean. In the beginning, I could concentrate very well and was in a pleasant state. However, after a period of time, things became more and more blurry and confusing. I do not know if this is a good way to meditate.

Venerable Master: Any wish to listen for a sound is a type of false thinking. This type of meditation is not transcendental in the truest sense, which is to be natural and free of greed, seeking, or anticipation. The exercise you describe involves wanting, and with wanting, you transcend nothing.

Question: So we should not think about anything?

Venerable Master:

A hundred things occur because one thought moves.

Ten thousand things cease when thought stops.
Quieting the mind brings real success.
Ending selfish desires creates real blessings.

Question: So, is transcendental meditation good or bad? It is now very popular in many countries around the world!

Venerable Master: Novel ways to meditate were created for those who cannot sit in the full lotus position. The fact is that we must learn to sit in full lotus to meditate. It is impossible to say that one has attained the Way without having sat in full lotus.

Question: The thing I am most sorry about is not having enough time to meditate.

Venerable Master: You must spare some time in your busy schedule and not waste it immersing yourself in confusion. You could cultivate at anytime and anywhere, not just by sitting there with your eyes closed.

Question: Where did Guanshiyin Bodhisattva come from?

Venerable Master: Ask yourself where you came from.

Question: While meditating in the last several days, the pain in my legs has intensified, especially in my left knee. This pain gradually rolled into a ball and stayed on my kneecap. When the pain heightened yesterday, it exploded and became a clean and warm energy that is yellow. It went from my knee to my ribs and to the upper part of my body. This warmth did not make me drowsy, but happy and comfortable. Later I saw a throne surrounded by white lotuses.

The edges to them seemed blurry, but their centers had purple buds like an inverted wine glass with a wide rim. They would suddenly change into mountains of gems, the bright lights of which are unprecedented. At times, they would also look like European castles or lotus daises like those upon which Bodhisattvas sit. There was a flat-headed snake that climbed to the top of the throne. Sometimes the scenes were transparent like a movie and would just flash by so I could not remember them well. I only remember that I seemed to be walking along on the seashore by myself. No one else was in sight. The place was quiet, beautiful, and charming. There was only the sound of seagulls that occasionally broke the silence. Now, I want to know if this was real or was it a result of my discriminating consciousness?

Venerable Master: Visions of Buddhas or flowers are not real when you have tried to visualize them and want to see them. Anything that you want to see is not real. The only significant state that is real is the one before a single thought occurs, though even that can be illusory at times. It is best not to encounter any state during meditation. There is nothing at all, just emptiness. Do not be shocked or happy. Reactions such as shock or happiness can cause you to become possessed by demons, as in the fifty skandha states listed in the *Shurangama Sutra*.

Question: Why should we meditate as we study the Buddhadharma?

Venerable Master: We meditate so that we can study a countless number of sutras and open the boundless wisdom inherent in our self-nature. There are countless Dharma-doors in our nature, but people tend to disregard the foundation and chase after the superficialities. We look for answers outside of ourselves, failing to realize that we should reflect.

Question: Please tell us again about the difference between entering samadhi and sleeping.

Venerable Master: During samadhi, a person remains very aware while sitting straight up.

His body does not move around and his head does not nod or tilt. This is the state of being still and yet always reflecting, reflecting and yet being always still. When asleep, you are not at all aware, you snore thunderously, and your position is completely the opposite of the stillness of samadhi.

170

Question: "It is better to study nothing for a day than to seek knowledge for a thousand days." What does this quote mean?

Venerable Master: "Not knowing when to quit the studying of different terms, we only trap ourselves by counting sand in the sea." *Who* is seeking knowledge for a thousand days? *Who* is studying nothing for a day? We should not keep on doing others' laundry.

Question: A kind of "Contemporary Chan" is popular now. I hear people achieve rather quick results with this. Master, is it okay to learn this "Contemporary Chan?"

Venerable Master: I am old fashioned and do not understand this contemporary question.

Question: While meditating, what should we be contemplating?

Venerable Master: Nothing specific. "Let your mind be nowhere." If there is anything specific, then you would be dwelling there. Dwell nowhere.

Question: Is there any difference between your method of meditation and that of Ajahn Sumedho? If so, how are they different?

Venerable Master: "There is only one path at the source, but there are many expedient entries." We are all people. Our faces look different. We all have minds, but we do not all think the same. You cannot make everyone uniform in every respect. The same principle applies here.

Question: Please briefly introduce meditation as it is taught at Gold Mountain Monastery.

Venerable Master: You will find out when you come to Gold Mountain Monastery. To begin with, we train ourselves to sit in the full lotus position. This position is called the *vajra* position, which can subdue demons.

Question: You just talked about how the full lotus posture is equivalent to a gold pagoda and a half lotus position is equivalent to a silver pagoda. Now, will you please discuss meditation?

Venerable Master: Do not be too anxious. You will only bite off more than you can chew. If you cannot sit in full lotus yet, sit in half lotus. The faster you want to go, the slower you will get where you want to go. Study one day at a time. You cannot graduate from college right away.

Question: How do we ask "Who is mindful of the Buddha?"

Venerable Master: You should investigate, "Who is mindful of the Buddha?" instead of asking it. Investigation is like drilling a hole. We will understand when we drill through. Before you do, you will not understand by asking the question. This method takes us to the point where language ceases to function and the mind stops thinking. No one can describe it. What others tell you is not it.

Question: It is generally said that the precepts help us enter samadhi and develop wisdom. Why does the Chan school only talk about cultivating a balance of samadhi and wisdom until we perfect our enlightenment and conduct?

Venerable Master: They can say whatever they want. It is also okay for some to talk only about precepts, or samadhi, or wisdom. It is not definite. It all depends on each individual's goals and principles. There is no set standard.

"White Universe"

Ice in the sky and snow on the ground
Cause countless tiny creatures
To die in the cold or sleep in hibernation.
Absorbed in stillness, contemplate.
While in movement, observe.
Dragons spar and tigers wrestle in continual playful sport.
Ghosts cry and spirits wail at weird illusory
transformations.
Ultimate truth transcends words and thought.
Proceed with haste.
When big and small are gone,
inside and outside cease to be.
Every little dust mote encompasses the Dharma Realm,
Complete, whole, and perfectly fused,
Interpenetrating and unobstructed.
With two clenched fists, shatter the covering of space.
In one mouthful, swallow the source of lands and seas.
Out of great compassion, use your own sweat and blood to
rescue all.
Never pause to rest!

-by Venerable Master Hua

8. VERSES ON CHAN AND CHAN POTENTIALS.

Clue about Chan Samadhi

Innocence found,
Vibrance abounds!
Thoughts turn straight and true.
Tame the mind. Let things go.
That is the vital clue.
As the earth dissolves,
Dualities will, too.
When space is shattered to smithereens,
Distinction-making will end.
A singular light then fills the cosmos.
Hold that pearl of wisdom.
Keep that mani gem close.
Transcending the defiled and pure,
Coming and going no longer occur.
The pulse will stop, thoughts, cease,
And the mad mind, be at peace.

February 21st, 1984
City of Ten Thousand Buddhas

Wonderful Truth In
Us All

When silence reigns, sounds cease,
And the countless conditions are quiet.
Then the boundless sky, the vast earth,
And all that is in between,
Unite with the Dharma Realm.
A single substance emerges.
Where did we come from to get here?
Where do we go when we leave?
In fact, neither you nor I exist.
Yet wonderful truth is in us all.
The wise will find it naturally.

December 27th, 1956

Topple Mount Sumeru

By knocking down Mount Sumeru
Obstacles are purged.
In the pure sea of our nature true,
No more waves emerge.
Awake, to penetrate and know
The true face of each of us.
Prajna wisdom always shows
That all things are forever thus.

Verse for starting the Chan session
Gold Mountain Chan Monastery, San Francisco

December 5th, 1971

An Intensive Course

Good people, scholars of sorts,
Gather here for an intensive course:
Study of the unconditioned.
In this arena, Buddhas come forth.
Whoever awakens earns honors.

Verse for starting the Chan session
Buddhist Lecture Hall, San Francisco

December 1969

Return of Spring

When spring gathers,
Things start to grow.
When space is shattered,
We come into our own.
Never again get fooled
By what self and others seem to be.
The Dharma Realm may be huge,
But it all fits within you and me.

Verse for starting the 98-day Chan session
Buddhist Lecture Hall, San Francisco

October 15th 1970

Self-portrait of Hsuan Hua
Sitting in Chan

Stilling thoughts is done in Dhyana.
A Bodhi sprout grows from *Mahaprajna*.
It needs to be tended with diligent care.
Awakening, with patience to bear
Insights about reality,
We are free to go and share
In the Dragon Flower Assembly.

Playing a Flute Without Holes

During an intensive Chan session,
Heaven and earth may be rent asunder.
Nor is it strange to get lessons,
In how to switch moons, in star plunder.
Standing before a shadowless peak,
A turn of the head will let you see.
Ever notice some true-blue soul
Playing a flute that has no holes?

Walk with Me

Upon awakening, do not be glad.
Before awakening, do not worry.
Work as hard as you ever have.
Hand-in-hand, walk with me.

Verse for ending the Chan session
Gold Mountain Chan Monastery, San Francisco

February 18th, 1972

Vajra Seed to Bodhi Sprout

Some time past, we sowed a vajra seed.
Our Bodhi sprout is now so tall it soars.
The fruit it bears will one day be
Instant awakening, proper and full,
Bringing us right to the Buddhas' door.

Verse for starting the Chan session
Buddhist Lecture Hall, San Francisco

September 12th, 1970

Who will there be?

Pick it up. Let it fall.
Who is mindful of the Buddha?
Ha! Ha! Ha!
Put it down. Can't let it go?
Who's the Buddha mindful of?
Ho! Ho! Ho!
It is not you. It is not me.
The two of us are two too many.
It is you, and it is me.
But when Sumeru topples,
Who will there be?

Verse for starting the Chan session
Gold Mountain Chan Monastery, San Francisco

March 11th, 1972

The Eighteen Great Vows of the Venerable Master Hua

On the nineteenth of the sixth lunar month, while practicing filial piety by his mother's grave, the Master made the following vows:

I bow before the Buddhas of the ten directions, the Dharma of the Tripitaka, and the holy Sangha of the past and present, praying that they will bear witness: I, disciple Tu Lun, An Tze, resolve not to seek for myself either the blessings of the gods or of humans, or the attainments of the Hearers, Those Enlightened by Conditions, or the Bodhisattvas of the Provisional Vehicle. Instead, I rely on the Supreme Vehicle, and bring forth the resolve for bodhi, vowing that all living beings in the Dharma Realm shall attain anuttara-samyak-sambodhi (Utmost Right and Perfect Enlightenment) at the same time as I.

1. I vow that I will not attain the Right Enlightenment if there is even one Bodhisattva in the ten directions and the three periods of time to the end of empty space

and the Dharma Realm who has not yet become a Buddha.

2. I vow that I will not attain the Right Enlightenment if there is even one Pratyekabuddha in the ten directions and the three periods of time to the end of empty space and the Dharma Realm who has not yet become a Buddha.

3. I vow that I will not attain the Right Enlightenment if there is even one Hearer in the ten directions and the three periods of time to the end of empty space and the Dharma Realm who has not yet become a Buddha.

4. I vow that I will not attain the Right Enlightenment if there is even one god in the Triple Realm who has not yet become a Buddha.

5. I vow that I will not attain the Right Enlightenment if there is even one human being in the worlds of the ten directions who has not yet become a Buddha.

6. I vow that I will not attain the Right Enlightenment if there is even one asura who has not yet become a Buddha.

7. I vow that I will not attain the Right Enlightenment

if there is even one animal who has not yet become a Buddha.

8. I vow that I will not attain the Right Enlightenment if there is even one hungry ghost who has not yet become a Buddha.

9. I vow that I will not attain the Right Enlightenment if there is even one being in the hells who has not yet become a Buddha.

10. I vow that I will not attain the Right Enlightenment if there is any being in the Triple Realm who has taken refuge with me and has not yet become a Buddha, be it a god, immortal, human being, or asura, a bird, aquatic creature, plant, or animal, a dragon, beast, ghost, or spirit.

11. I vow to bestow upon all beings of the Dharma Realm all the blessings and happiness I am destined to receive.

12. I vow to take upon myself all the miseries of all living beings of the Dharma Realm, that I alone may endure them on their behalf.

13. I vow that my spirit shall enter the hearts

of all living beings who do not believe in the Buddhadharma, causing them to reform their evil conduct and practice the good, repent of their errors and start anew, take refuge with the Triple Jewel, and ultimately realize Buddhahood.

14. I vow that every living being who has seen my face or even heard my name will bring forth the Bodhi resolve and quickly realize the Buddha Way.

15. I vow to respectfully observe the Buddha's instructions and take only one meal a day and that at noon.

16. I vow to enlighten all sentient beings according to their dispositions.

17. I vow in this very life to attain the Five Eyes and Six Spiritual Powers, and the ability to fly freely.

18. I vow that my vows will all be fulfilled.

I vow to save the numberless living beings.
I vow to eradicate the inexhaustible afflictions.
I vow to study the limitless Dharma-doors.
I vow to realize the supreme Buddha Way.

Dharma Realm Buddhist Association Branches

World Headquarters

The City of Ten Thousand Buddhas
2001 Talmage Road
Ukiah, CA 95482 USA
tel: (707) 462-0939
fax: (707) 462-0949
www.drba.org
(Branch URLs and email addresses are available on the DRBA website.)

U.S.A.
California
Berkeley

Berkeley Buddhist Monastery
2304 McKinley Avenue
Berkeley, CA 94703 USA
tel: (510) 848-3440
fax: (510) 548-4551

Burlingame

The International Translation Institute
1777 Murchison Drive
Burlingame, CA 94010-4504 USA
tel: (650) 692-5912
fax: (650) 692-5056

Long Beach

Blessings, Prosperity, and Longevity Monastery
4140 Long Beach Boulevard
Long Beach, CA 90807 USA
tel/fax: (562) 595-4966

Long Beach Sagely Monastery
3361 East Ocean Boulevard
Long Beach, CA 90803 USA
tel: (562) 438-8902

Los Angeles

Gold Wheel Monastery
235 North Avenue 58
Los Angeles, CA 90042 USA
tel: (323) 258-6668
fax: (323) 258-3619

Sacramento

The City of the Dharma Realm
1029 West Capitol Avenue
West Sacramento, CA 95691 USA
tel: (916) 374-8268
fax: (916) 374-8234

San Francisco

Gold Mountain Monastery
800 Sacramento Street
San Francisco, CA 94108 USA
tel: (415) 421-6117
fax: (415) 788-6001

San Jose

Gold Sage Monastery
11455 Clayton Road
San Jose, CA 95127 USA
tel: (408) 923-7243
fax: (408) 923-1064

Maryland
Bethesda

Avatamsaka Vihara
9601 Seven Locks Road
Bethesda, MD 20817-9997 USA
tel/fax: (301) 469-8300

Washington
Index

Snow Mountain Monastery
PO Box 272
50924 Index-Galena Road
Index, WA 98256 USA
tel: (360) 799-0699
fax: (815) 346-9141

Seattle

Gold Summit Monastery
233 1st Avenue
West Seattle, WA 98119 USA
tel: (206) 284-6690

Canada
Alberta

Avatamsaka Monastery
1009 4th Avenue
S.W. Calgary, AB T2P OK, Canada
tel: (403) 234-0644

British Columbia

Gold Buddha Monastery
248 East 11th Avenue
Vancouver, B.C. V5T 2C3, Canada
tel: (604) 709-0248
fax: (604) 684-3754

Australia

Gold Coast Dharma Realm
106 Bonogin Road
Bonogin, Queensland AU 4213
Australia
tel: 61-755-228-788
fax: 61-755-227-822

Hong Kong

Buddhist Lecture Hall
31 Wong Nei Chong Road, Top Floor
Happy Valley, Hong Kong, China
tel: (852) 2572-7644
fax: (852) 2572-2850

Cixing Chan Monastery
Lantou Island, Man Cheung Po
Hong Kong, China
tel: (852) 2985-5159

Malaysia

Dharma Realm Guanyin Sagely Monastery
Prajna Guanyin Sagely Monastery
161, Jalan Ampang
50450 Kuala Lumpur, Malaysia
tel: (603) 2164-8055
fax: (603) 2163-7118

Fa Yuan Monastery
1 Jalan Utama
Taman Serdang Raya
43300 Seri Kembangan
Selangor Darul Ehsan, Malaysia
tel: (603) 8948-5688

Malaysia DRBA Penang Branch
32-32C, Jalan Tan Sri Teh Ewe Lim
11600 Jelutong
Penang, Malaysia
tel: (604) 281-7728
fax: (604) 281-7798

Guan Yin Sagely Monastery
166A Jalan Temiang
70200 Seremban
 Negeri Sembilan, Malaysia
tel/fax: (606)761-1988

Lotus Vihara
136, Jalan Sekolah
45600 Batang Berjuntai
Selangor, Malaysia
tel: (603) 3271- 9439

Taiwan

Dharma Realm Buddhist Books Distribution Society
11th Floor, 85 Zhongxiao E. Road, Sec. 6
Taipei 115, Taiwan R.O.C.
tel: (02) 2786-3022
fax: (02) 2786-2674

Dharma Realm Sagely Monastery
No. 20, Dongxi Shanzhuang
Liugui Dist.
Gaoxiong 844, Taiwan, R.O.C.
tel: (07) 689-3717
fax: (07) 689-3870

Amitabha Monastery
No. 136, Fuji Street, Chinan Village, Shoufeng
Hualian County 974, Taiwan, R.O.C.
tel: (03) 865-1956
fax: (03) 865-3426

Subsidiary Organizations

Buddhist Text Translation Society
City of Ten Thousand Buddhas
4951 Bodhi Way, Ukiah. CA 95482 USA
web: www.buddhisttexts.org
email: info@buddhisttexts.org
catalog: www.bttsonline.org

Dharma Realm Buddhist University
City of Ten Thousand Buddhas
4951 Bodhi Way, Ukiah, CA 95482 USA
www.drbu.org

Dharma Realm Outreach
City of Ten Thousand Buddhas
outreach@drba.org

Instilling Goodness and Developing Virtue School
City of Ten Thousand Buddhas
2001 Talmage Road, Ukiah, CA 95482 USA
www.igdvs.org

Institute for World Religions
2245 McKinley Avenue, Suite B
Berkeley, CA 94703 USA
web: www.drbu.org/iwr
email: iwr@drbu.org

Religion East & West (journal)
2245 McKinley Avenue, Suite B
Berkeley, CA 94703 USA
tel: 510-848-9788
web: www.drbu.org/iwr/rew

Vajra Bodhi Sea (magazine)
Gold Mountain Monastery
800 Sacramento Street
San Francisco, CA 94108 USA
tel: (415) 421-6117
fax: (415) 788-6001